Historical guide to
Biggar High Street

This book is dedicated to the late Brian Lambie MBE,
ironmonger, provost and museum director
whose research, collections and reminiscences form the foundation of this publication

Published 2022

Text, maps, drawings, tables © Jim Ness unless otherwise attributed.

All rights reserved.
The rights of Jim Ness to be identified as author of this work under the Copyright, Design and Patent Act 1988.

ISBN 978-1-3999-2208-1

Printed by Elmbank Print Peebles   www.elmbankprint.co.uk

Contents

Introduction	1
South side, numbers 2-184	4
Key to building numbers	5
Park Place	46
North side, numbers 1-227	46
Kirkstyle	58
Appendices	91
Bibliography	92
Acknowledgements	92
List of businesses 1886, 1986	93

a layout in topological form but the Kirk, High Street and many closes can be defined.

Biggar, along with Lanark and Peebles, fits the model of a Scottish market town in having a wide main street rather than a market square at the centre. Kelso is the most notable exception to this. The first cartographically accurate depiction comes in 1858 when the Ordnance Survey produced its 25 inch to the mile plans.

Up to the late 1700s the High St was much wider than it appears now. The greater width accommodated a multitude of markets described later. This has greatly altered the appearance of the south side of the street but many of the original front buildings still exist behind the current frontage e.g. at Weir Court. Buildings started to encroach on the street in the early nineteenth century and by 1900 the present layout would have been largely recognisable.

The New Statistical Account of 1835 noted the following inventory of annual shop sales in the town: 2608 gallons British spirit (whisky), 80 gallons brandy, 136 gallons ginger wine, 88 dozen foreign wines, 2528 lbs tea, 1876 lbs tobacco and snuff. From 1841 census returns give us names and businesses but not necessarily exact locations for them. Some of the trades still flourishing in 1841 included horse dealer, thatcher, rat catcher, cotton hand-loom weaver and toll keeper.

Most of the buildings are in the vernacular style utilising plum whinstone rubble and sandstone rybats. The whinstone, a volcanic andesite, was quarried on the Knock, each nineteenth and early twentieth century builder having his own quarry and the sandstone brought from Libberton. A few buildings were constructed from a blue-green sandstone from the quarry on Broughton road and at least one from Bizzyberry rhyolite – a very difficult stone to work. Many of the buildings are cherry-cock-pointed using small stones to fill the gaps between the larger blocks. After the arrival of the railway in 1860 it became feasible to use a finer freestone from Locharbriggs in Dumfriesshire on buildings such as the Post Office.

In 1862 William Hunter in 'Biggar and the House of Fleming' noted encroachment of new buildings onto the High Street, the middens and peat stacks of old had disappeared but he thought the scene could be improved by the removal of piles of wood and rubbish. The peat stacks were so common as the townsfolk had the right to extract peat from Biggar Moss but by the 1840s most had given up these rights. Dr Aiton of Dolphinton in a speech of the same year described having seen Biggar for the first time around 1820 – *'a splendid panorama of peat stacks, and huts of every dimension, standing all reel-ral as if fallen from the clouds.'* 1862 also saw the passing of Provost Lindsay's Act allowing for the election of officers who would oversee the installation of street

101	G Wilson	Baker	Coffee Garden	Café
107	J Archibald	Grocer	Brownlies	Grocer
109-11	R Russell	Crown Inn	Crown Inn	
113			This Is It	Health Foods
117	AR Dickson	Draper	Sheena Rae	Wool
119	Jas Porteous	Grocer	Thorpe	Garden sundries
119	D Hunter		Thorpe	Garden sundries
119	John Gladstone	Ironmonger	Thorpe	Garden sundries
123	John Vallance	Saddler	Wm Paul	Greengrocer
125	Roderick McKay	Commercial Inn	Private house	
129	John Affleck	Saddler	Chocolate Box	
131	David Lockhart, Jas B Watson	Printer	Gift Box	
133	Jas Wyld	Grocer	Braedale Electrical	
139	W Johnson	Draper	Lennard's	Shoes
143	Mrs Sinclair	Fleming Arms	Fleming Arms	
143	D Murray	Draper and Cycle Agent	Fleming Arms	
145-7	Mrs Cook	Elphinstone Inn	Elphinstone Hotel	
153	W Ovens	Grocer	Bryden	Stationer
155	Alex Russell	Shoemaker	Bill Brown	Travel
157				Vet
161	J Johnson	Baker	Kelly	Hairdresser
165	Mrs Core	Coffee House		
169	J Rae	Shoemaker	Norah Thomson	Clothes
171	D Lawson	Grocer	Ovens	Butcher
181			Social Club	
183			Taylor's	Ice cream factory
187	Joseph Poletti	China merchant	Townhead café	
209	Geo Pillans, Mrs Brunton	Tailor	Asif Foodstore	Grocer

	1886		1986	
1-3 Park Pl	Wm Johnstone	Draper	Oriental	Restaurant
7 Park Pl	Mrs Inglis	Grocer	J Simpson	Fishmonger
1-3	Wm Lamb	Cross Keys	Cross Keys	Public house
7-9	Jas Niven	Draper	Sheila Conn	Clothes
15	Gilbert Rae	Ironmonger	Jean Attwood	Clothes
17	Graham	Butcher	J Hamilton	Butcher
19	Post Office			
25	Wm Low	Draper	WJ Simpson	Footware
27-29	Jas Wilson	Baker	Knitwise	
33			Continental Delicatessan	Food
35	D Mitchell	Watchmaker	J&W Dunn	Solicitors and accountants
39			T O'Donnell	Paint Shop
47	Marion Lauder	Toyshop		
55			Antiques (vacant)	
63	Proctor and Weir	Plumbers	Alliance; Braxfield	Bdg Soc; insurance
67	Geo Mitchell	Saddler	Jenny Wren	Crafts
69	John G Brown	Jeweller (1903)	Yuill (vacant)	Jeweller
77-79	National Bank		Smail and Ewart	Solicitors
81	Adam Pairman	Draper	Gladstone and Core	Draper
			GN Pomphrey	Solicitors
87	Jas Stephen	Plumbers	Anglia	Building Soc
89	W Alcock	Printer	Woolen Mill	
93	W Scott	Butcher	Brown Bros	Butcher; delicatessen,freezer ctr
99	W Rae	Shoemaker	Gibson	Baker

84	Miss Jeannie McMath	Grocer	Wilson	Grocer
86	Robt M Dickson	Draper	JD Brown	Draper
88	W Rae	Shoemaker	JD Brown	Draper
92	W Lindsay	Painter		
96	Jas Adams	Barber	New Image	Hairdresser
100	R Murray	Tailor	Floral Gift Centre	
104	D Thomson	Royal Bank	Royal Bank	
110	Jas Gibson	Meal merchant	Fish Restaurant	
114	Wm Hislop	Watchmaker	Ritchie	Electrician
116	Walter Brunton	Butcher	Biggar Wines	Off License
120	Robt Boa	Ironmonger	Robt Boa	Ironmonger
122	Jas Masterton	Builder		
124	Teenie Ling	Home made toffee balls	Corner Shop	
	Corn Exchange		Corn Exchange	
128	Robt Clark	Joiner		
128	D and M Aitken	Slaters		
138			A Weir	Plumber
142	Thos Harlan			Garage
144	Geo Stringer	Painter		Clothes
146	Geo Cook	Grocer		
152	Geo Wilson	Joiner	M Aitken	Slater
154			Gold Cup	Carry-out restaurant
156	Alex Weir	Blacksmith	Stephens of Biggar	Garage
176	Geo Tweedie	Joiner	W&M Lethan	Clothes

Appendices

From the Poetical Works of James Afflek—

ADDRESS OF THE RATS AND MICE

TO TWO DISPUTANTS WHO HAD DISAGREED ABOUT A
BARGAIN OF OAT-MEAL, WHICH WAS DEPOSITED,
BY AN ORDER OF THE SHERIFF, IN THE MEAL
HOUSE, BIGGAR, UNTIL THE PLEA THEN
PENDING SHOULD BE SETTLED

We, a company of Rats, lodgers in the Meal House, Biggar, by the special advice and consent of the mice, do herein, hereon, and hereat, testify our most grateful and sincere thanks to Mr Nicol Porteous, Toll-keeper, and Mr William Brechen, Baker, for their hearty difference which had been attended with very happy consequences to us. We are glad to learn that pride continues to swell each bosom; be it therefore known to the world that meal shall swell our bellies. Gentlemen, hold fast your integrity, and nothing shall terrify us; we have for a time been supported by the law, and, like our hungry brethren in Lanark, hope still to be.

1890 Public buildings – Commercial bank, 1836; National bank, 1863; Gillespie Church, 1878; Post office, 1898; Royal bank, 1852, Corn Exchange, 1861; Freemason's Hall, 1814.

1890 Advertisers, Crocket – Wm Ovens, grocer, opp Corn Exchange; Thos MacFarlane, chemist and aerated water manufacturer; David Dickson, butcher; Geo Wilson, baker; JB Watson, stationer, pianos for hire; Alex Russell, bootmaker; Michell, watchmaker, West End; Mrs Geo Kelly, fish and greengrocer, West End; Rae, Gladstone and Brown, ironmongers; Water Rae, bootmaker; Jas Watson, temperance hotel, few doors from Corn Exchange (White Hart); David Murray, draper and cycle merchant. John Brownlie, grocer; Jas Wilson, West End Tea and Coffee Rooms; Wm Linton, grocer; Lindsay bros, painters; Wm Hislop, watchmaker and Jeweller; Elphinstone Hotel, Mrs Cook; John Archibald, grocer; Robt Russell, butcher; John Eunson, chemist; John Rae, bootmaker, John Graham, baker; Mrs C Brunton (late Jas Brunton), grocer, West End; A Brown, photographer; John Johnston, baker, East End; Thos Watson, bootmaker; Anne Inglis, grocer, West End; Thos Harlan, painter, West End; JN Abernethy, butcher, West End; David Lawson, grocer, East End.

Aug 1913 Advertisers by JH Wilson, printer and stationer.

Stephens Motor Garage (opp PO). Ford agents. Bicycles for sale.

John Eunson, Chemist. Dark room for developing and printing photos for amateurs.

Donald Adams, hairdresser, tobacconist, fishing tackle dealer.

Gillespie church, Rev AP Muirhead

Banks – Royal, Commercial, National (WB Pairman)

Post Office – postmaster A Provan

John Graham, butcher - High St near fountain and Victoria Place, West End

John Brunton – grocer and wine merchant

Mrs Kelly – fishmonger and poulterer, Victoria Place, West End

Archibald Bogle – fish merchant, Main St opposite Royal Bank

JS Dempster – photographic apparatus and chemicals. Dark room. Chemist.

Bow's Well was the subject of controversy in December 1884. John McGhie, a burgh commissioner, had condemned the burgh wells as the water supply was deemed to be impure and he engaged one of James Stephen's plumbers to remove the handles from the pumps. The poor plumber was set upon by a mass of 'East-end Amazons' demonstrating for women's' rights. Their nearest water supply would have been from the burn 500 yards away. Further attempts to remove the handles of other wells were met by the population in confiscating the handles themselves much to McGhie's chagrin. Effigies of the unfortunate commissioner and one of his acolytes were later burned by a crowd at the head of a torch-lit protest procession. The episode led to the installation of a new water supply from the King's Beck on Culter Fell in 1885. 221 was the locus of Andrew Leith's oil merchant's business in the 1940s and he continued van deliveries previously delivered by his father-in-law James Kerr on Kerr's retiral.

The semi-detached two-storey block at **Nos 225-7** was built c.1935 and was notable for having smooth rendering with sickle shaped depressions applied to the surface. No 227 was the home of John Proudfoot, one of the town's postmen, whose prize begonias in his greenhouse brightened the north-eastern approach to the town.

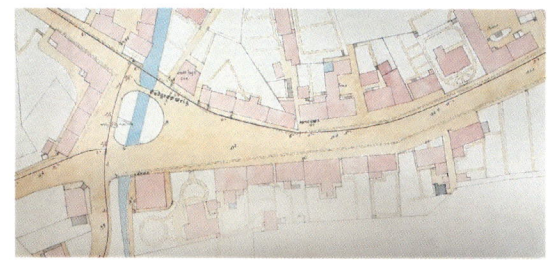

Plans of the Burgh of Biggar, 1885

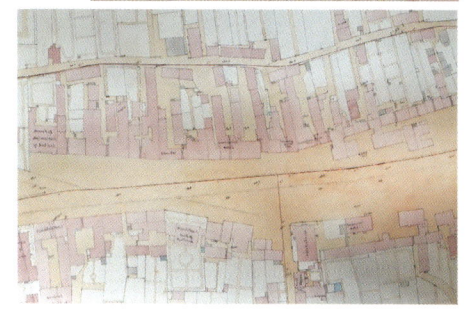

An early, probably 1860s, view of the East End beyond Townhead from Nos 213 to 221. Bow's well and the old toll gate are visible towards the right.

a pump on the Ordnance Survey 1st Edition map of 1858) which had been occupied by John, 11th Lord Elphinstone after Boghall Castle had fallen into disrepair. It had also been occupied by Bailie Thomas Carmichael around 1744 who died in 1785 aged eighty-two.

afterwards it was sold to Charlie Caffola and the Lido Café set up business here then Con Ricci in the 1930s and '40s with his prize winning ice-cream and it has been a focus for refreshment and sustenance ever since. Con continued the business along with the Corner Café until his death in 1964. The Polettis continued to live in the upstairs flat for some time after the Caffolas bought the business. They used one of their rooms as the Roman Catholic chapel before Breezehill on Coulter Road became St Isodore's and it was the home of the priest, Thomas McDonna in 1901. Masses were also held by Fr George Mason, the RC chaplain at the Talla Reservoir construction site.

The area in front of **Nos 193-205** was excavated by the Biggar Archaeology Group in 1999. The excavation revealed, beneath 19th century finds, the presence of 17th and 18th century clay pipe stems and green glaze and Staffordshire pottery. There was also a large quantity of shattered slate, but none with holes, indicating a possible roofing slate preparation site.

No 195 was the home of the Selkirk family in 1900. There is a seventeenth century lintel built into the front wall which reads 16 . WG . MT . ЯS . 91

Nos 207, 209. Plans exist for Mr Noble's shop and house at East End adjoining his house in 1871. A datestone of 1847 above a window lintel is from an earlier building. George Pillans a grocer and tailor worked there up to February 1894 and it seems to have been a shared location with Margaret Brunton the grocer as she was there up to the 1920s. From the late 1930s Robert Elliot, Mr Slimmon, RJ Scott and TA McGarry had the grocer's business up to the late twentieth century.

No 213. Dalmore, the dental surgery was the home of Andrew Hope the builder who gave his name to the adjoining close. The area in front was known as the golden sands in the early twentieth century due to the yellow gravel neatly laid down by Mrs Hope in front of the house.

No 215 – 217 is an eighteenth century house with a circular rear stair which was renovated by the Burgh Council in the 1950s. Four separate houses were combined into one at the same time. Up to 1948 No 217 had been the business of John Poletti, plumber and domestic engineer when Angus McMillan took over. The showroom was on North Back Road.

No 219 was the home of Bailie John Robertson, 1773-1864, the last baron bailie of Biggar. Robertson was responsible for the distribution of ale to the drouthy at the corse knowe to celebrate Queen Victoria's coronation in 1838. Mr Melvin ran a transport accommodation business from here in the 1950s.

No 221. Hunter in *Biggar and the House of Fleming* describes a house in this location, just down from Bow's Well (shown as

The rear of Nos 215-7 before restoration in the 1950s

business to be succeeded by his son, William Otto who was born in Sanquhar in 1802 and died in Biggar in 1849. The latter married the Baron Baillie and builder's daughter Annie Robertson. Some of Reid's clocks still exist and many of his works are preserved in The Museum of Biggar and Upper Clydesdale.

Nos 167, 169 and 171 are on site of a fortalice, a small fortified house for the defence of the town, possibly pre-dating Boghall Castle. It belonged to James Brown and was his legacy to the Rev Alexander Livingstone and some kirk elders of Biggar Kirk in 1659 to be used as a schoolhouse and its rental being paid into the burgh poor fund. A carved lintel, now harled over, survives from around this time. It is carved with the words 'Ora et labora ut floreant studia – 1691' – 'Pray and work to make study flourish'. It was sold by the Kirk Session in 1774 and fell into the hands of Richard Johnston and his wife Agnes (Nannie) Muir. It was an establishment where drinking, dancing and fighting whiles prevailed but Nannie ruled her hostelry with a commanding hand. A photograph of the 1870s shows Robert Thomson, grocer in 169 and to the right Robert Gibson, draper in what is now 171. David Lawson also had a grocery at 171 from May 1892 and expanded in 1899. It later accommodated Matthew Robertson. The back shop of 169 belonged to John Rae, father of the poet and ironmonger Gilbert Rae, a shoemaker who lived from 1843 to 1933. He employed three men on the site in 1871. His brother, Walter, was also a shoemaker. The Raes had a confectioner and fruiterer's shop in the 1940s.

The area to the east, **Howieson Square**, was named after the Howieson family who owned part of it from the 1850s.

Nos 185-191. The Townhead Café building was built on site of a tenement with its gable to the street, home to James Affleck, tailor and poet. Born in Drumelzier in 1776, he was apprenticed to Gilbert Tait establishing as a master tailor in Biggar in 1793. Several volumes of poetry including a collaboration with artist John Pairman in 1817 were published. He died in 1835, aged 59, and is buried in Biggar Kirkyard. Hunter described his poetry as 'indifferent' and Antiquarius in 1843 as 'poor fizenless doggrel' but he was Biggar's makar, writing rhymes to celebrate all sorts of local events, full of anecdotes and shrewd observations. In his role as Masonic Chaplain in 1832 he adopted a poetic style and he was a great favourite in the all the houses he sewed in with his stories and recitations. The demon drink however was to torment Affleck and may have contributed to his death. From the 1860s the building had been the home and business of the Polettis, a family of Italian origin via Dunning in Perthshire. Joseph Poletti, b. Italy, 1774 had been a barometer maker. He became Biggar's oldest resident dying in 1872 at the age of 98. Joseph Jr ran a china shop and mobile service which included a rag and bone collection till his death in June 1900. Shortly

These two images were taken on the same day around 1870. Top Nos 167-191 – Thomson, grocer, Gibson, draper and Poletti's china shop.

Bottom from No 144- possibly in Ovens's time, The White Hart, Corn Exchange back across to Poletti's.

No 161 – Carruther's Townhead Bakery c.1910 with Fraser Whitefield, Alan Thomson, Robert Carruthers and John Lindsay.

Elephants of the Bostock and Wombwell menagerie making friends on the High Street.

back on the right hand side. Robert died in 1863 and shortly afterwards his widow established a coffee house and the legend 'Mrs Core's Coffee House' was painted in bold letters across the building. (It was still faintly noticeable until the wall paint got thicker). Their son, Tom Core, a partner with William Gladstone at No 81 stayed here. Mr GP Main, a native of Carnwath was there in the mid-twentieth century and was for a long time the only dentist in the town, occasionally assisted by his son James. He used the cobbler's workshop and the front room on the right, upstairs as a surgery. Before Core this was Reid the watchmaker's place. Andrew Reid was born around 1767 and lived till 1860. He built up the

ran Biggar's first savings bank from the shop from 1832. By 1850 it had 630 depositors with funds in excess of £5,000. Sums from 1/- to £10 could be deposited. He was also one of the founders of the Biggar Bible Association. The association was responsible for producing large-print versions of the bible for the poorly sighted and French and Spanish versions for the 300 or so post-Napoleonic prisoners-of-war held in Biggar. Pairman became fluent in French. They also published a Gaelic version for the many casual highland labourers in the district but sadly none of them were able to read. In 1850 William Ovens took over (he claimed that the business was established in 1806) and the name continued until 1946. In 1884 he proudly advertised the fact that the Analytical Laboratory of Surgeon's Hall, Edinburgh deemed his whisky blend to have a fully-developed ethereal bouquet and was in first class condition. Ovens made the building stand out by having a set of iron railings installed around the first floor. Ovens had managed the building of the Moat Park church in 1865. Jimmy Tennent ran the business from the First World War and gave his name to the adjacent close. Tennant was followed by a partnership between James Kerr and his daughter, Mrs S Murray and after that John Fergus. Bryden's newsagent's moved there in 1946.

A date stone of 1771 is built in at the back of **No155**. William Russell came to Biggar from Carnwath around 1824 and set up a shoe and boot making business. Russell was a devoted abstainer and a leading member of the temperance league. He would later buy the White Hart Inn opposite and have it run as a temperance hotel. He was an elder in the United Presbyterian Church and died in 1884. Alex, his son was at 155 in the 1880s. Alex Clark had the business in the early twentieth century and James Johnston in the 1940s. Clark had inherited the house from Mr Watson, another shoemaker who died in 1898, and his family. The Watson daughters ran a temperance coffee house in the Corn Exchange on fair days as an alternative to the refreshments offered by the public houses. They were also responsible for planting the elm trees at Moat Park. The building later became a grocer's and the Tourist Information Office.

Nos 157 and 159, Johnstone Square. Additions between the front and back houses were made by James Hepburn, a baker in 1865.

No 161 was the business of J Johnstone the baker in the 1880s and '90s followed by R Carruthers when it was called the Townhead Bakery. Robert Elliot the grocer was there in the 1950s and '60s and it had a short spell as Zanussi's Italian chip shop in the 1940s. **No165** was occupied by Robert Core (1810-63) the cobbler in the mid-19th century. There is a photograph of him in a bowling club group of 1859. His workshop, where he employed five men, was in the room at the

cess to the stables. Here was the booking office for carriage hiring, Jimmy Dickson being the trap and charabanc driver in the early twentieth century. The business survived the occupancy of the Hare family from 1904 but was enhanced in the 1930s when the Harveys painted the facade green and cream. Following the Harveys came the Cochranes, Dilworths and the Barrie family in 1958. In 1970 the frontage was given a face-lift to conform to the Civic Trust Street Improvement Scheme and was restored to black and white. The heraldic sign introduced by the Harvies was repainted by A Stevenson with the arms of the Elphinstone family. As with the town's other pubs, the Elph bar has many a tale to tell.

Grace Carrick relates the following about Smug Smith: *'Old Smug in his late years had become the worse for wear due probably to the drink he had consumed over his lifetime and was a regular visitor to all the pubs and hotels in the town, carrying with him his ivory bagpipes and in previous years with friend Jimmy Vance who played the fiddle they would entertain customers for payment in kind of beer and whisky. As age caught up with him he became rather dishevelled in his dress and frequented the bar in the Elphinstone hotel, often sitting in front of the coal fire which glowed and permeated heat. Unfortunately old Smug also started to permeate a terrible smell which got so bad regular customers began to complain to the owner's wife, who fed up at getting complaints asked her husband to have a word with old Smug. Not wanting to appear unkind he said "Now Smug, can ye not tidy yourself up and have a clean, because if you don't I'm afraid I'll need to ban you from the pub!" This didn't go down well with Smug who left and went home to his cottage further up the town and donned his good black funeral suit and white shirt, kept especially for that occasion, combed his long wax handlebar moustache and returned to the pub. Much to everyone's surprise including the owner Smug appeared looking very dapper, his makeover obviously making an impression on those looking on. "Come in, come in Smug" said the owner "My goodness what a difference, now what do you want to drink?" "Drink! Drink! in here said Smug "A widnae be seen deid in a dump like this!" and walked out, having made his point!'*

A fuller history of the Elphinstone Hotel written by Brian Lambie can be read on the hotel's website.

No153 sits on the site of an old tenement or shared building projecting out onto the street inhabited, amongst others, by William Borthwick, a bookbinder. Borthwick was infamous for firing a gun at a cobbler, William Gall, at foot of Canongate Close (Smith's Close) where Gall fell but to no harm. Borthwick, however thought he'd killed him and fled only to be found and taken home to his weeping wife. Another resident of the same tenement almost destroyed it. She had been accused by a neighbour of stealing from his peat stack so he packed one of his peats with gunpowder. Some peat was duly stolen, put on her fire and the peat blew up in front of her whilst toasting feet and sent her head over heels in the air. She lived to tell the tale and learned her lesson. The tenement survived until 1806 when Robert Pairman (1784-1867), the brother of John Pairman the artist and father of the doctor, started his grocer's business with cellars beneath. Robert's grandson, Thomas, recalled being mesmerised by a Christmas tree bedecked with little candles – the first in Biggar. On one occasion Robert had ordered a barrel of treacle directly from Jamaica. The barrel was tapped but the liquid treacle only flowed very slowly. On opening the barrel it was found to contain the body of a Jamaican man! Pairman

From No 137 – Falkland House, John Sinclair's Fleming Arms, Mrs Cook's Elphinstone Hotel and William Ovens grocery in the 1880s.

since the 1860s and exhibited their animals on the Cross Knowe site. Animals included Wallace the veteran lion and the bell-ringing Mafeking monkey. A 1905 visit 'exhibited' an eighteen-year-old, thirty-stone Hungarian boy!

By 1850 the name 'Stewart's Inn' appeared and Archibald Campbell was the inn keeper with his wife, brother, young son and cook Christina Forrest. Campbell hired out horses, a hearse and ran a shuttle coach to Symington Station to meet the Glasgow and Edinburgh trains. Anthony Wilson owned the hotel in 1855 and David Thomson briefly took over in 1869. Janet Cook had managed the hotel from 1865, and become owner in 1869. Under her management the inn continued to prosper and became the scene of many important local functions and dinners. She ran a soup kitchen (Biggar's first food bank?) in 1879 with the aid of public subscriptions. In September 1902 however Mrs Cook was fined 1/- at the Justice of the Peace Court for having sold a Mr Marshbanks a pint of beer whilst already intoxicated!

A distinguishing feature of the inn in those days was an archway (situated where the public bar is now), which gave ac-

To the east of Smith's Close is **Falkland House, Nos 137 and 139**. It was named after the Falkland Islands to where an early occupant had relations emigrate. In 1820 it was the locus of John Pairman the draper and later portrait artist. Pairman moved to Edinburgh to work and cashed in on portrait work before photography did away with what had been a lucrative trade. He died in 1843. William Johnston, a draper and clothier was there till February 1893 along with DG Murray. George Weir was a grocer there in 1905.

Next door is the **Fleming Arms** combining **Nos 141 and 143** but the present public bar space was until the mid-twentieth century a separate shop. In the 1880s, when wagonettes and dog carts could be hired from the premises, John Sinclair was the publican and his sign still exists behind the current inn sign. James Frame became the proprietor in the late 1930s followed by Joe Todd and Jackie Tickle in the 1950s. Todd had his hotel license reduced to that of a public house in 1960 after several complaints about the lack of coffee and meals available. Occupants of the shop included in the 1880s James Gibson and David G Murray, draper, clothier and cycle agent, Robert Hunter till 1897 and J Graham, both cabinetmakers and by 1920 the Buttercup Dairy. Murray, the cycle agent sold, along with national brands, his own range of 'Challenge' cycles. The buildings to the rear of the Fleming Arms were until the 1960s the home of Biggar Fire Brigade.

145, 147 The Elphinstone Hotel. The 'Elph' as it is affectionately known has been around since at least the eighteenth century. Known then as Workmen's Inn (after a family name) and later The Wigtoun Arms, owing to the feudal superior Fleming family of Boghall being also Earls of Wigtoun, it was run by the Wilson family after a disposition by James Bertram in 1808. The name became 'Elphinstone' when the Fleming male line ran out and Lord Elphinstone inherited the Fleming estates. Hunter, in 1862, refers to the Elphinstone Arms and Wigtoun Arms as two separate establishments but neither the 1861 census nor the Ordnance Survey of 1858 mention the Wigtoun Arms.

A visitor of 1878, Captain Robert Riddell, refers to the hostelry as "a tolerable good inn". In the 1830s and '40s the inn was a principal posting house on the road from Edinburgh to Carlisle. Horses on private carriages had to be changed regularly and the Elphinstone was one of the coaching inns where horses were changed. Boom years occurred between 1848 and 1864 when carriages shuttled visitors from the Caledonian Railway station at Symington to the Biggar hotels. The Elph attracted more customers than the others by the enticement of a glass of whisky. In the early twentieth century the rear stables were managed by Sandy Howieson and the old pre-motor town hearse was garaged in the Elphinstone stables until the 1930s. Their stables had a much more exotic use in 1922 when they were used to house the camels and elephants of the Bostock and Wombwell menagerie when it came to Biggar en route from Moffat to the Kelvin Hall carnival in Glasgow. B&W had been visiting Biggar

Re-painting of the Fleming Arms in 1988 revealed Mrs Sinclair's sign of 1936. Murray's sign may date from the 1880s.

1868 - north side of the High Street from lamp-post rightwards – National Bank; Adam Pairman, draper; Stephen, tinsmith; A Doggart, printer; Scott, butcher; J Graham, baker; W Rae, shoemaker; G Wilson, baker; Archibald, grocer; Toward, Crown; draper; grocer (white apron); J Gladstone, ironmonger (26) in doorway; Vallance, saddler; Kennedy, Commercial Inn; Lodge 167; Affleck, saddler; D Lockhart, printer (at his door); Jas Wyld, Royal Insurance Office, grocer.

the 1860s, Affleck the saddler was there and Carruthers the bookseller and stationer in the 1890s.

Nos 131-133 was the site in the seventeenth, eighteenth and early nineteenth centuries of Craig, the baker's. Title deeds from around 1680 are in the name of this family and they went on to buy several other plots of land around the town. There is extant a handbill of 1825 for William Borthwick, bookseller at this location. The present two-storey edifice was built around 1843. At **No 131** was the business of D Lockhart, bookseller, printer and Hamilton Advertiser correspondent in the early 1890s and Watson the printer and stationer by 1898. Lockhart is recorded in 1855 valuation rolls and published 'Biggar and the House of Fleming' in 1862. His premises included a reading room which was well-stocked with newspapers and magazines and much appreciated in the community. He was a lieutenant in the local volunteer corps but had to resign when he accidentally shot the marker, Tom Pairman in 1875. He was also Biggar's registrar and ironically he had to register Pairman's death which he had caused. D and M Penman had a sweet shop there in the 1950s and later Messrs Leckie and Ford. Adam Wyld had bought **No 133** before 1841. Wyld ran a hardware store and was an agent for the Royal Insurance Company and the store name ran on through the nineteenth century. He was succeeded by his wife and son, James followed by William Linton the grocer in 1891 and Alex Smith by 1907 who gave his name to the adjacent Smith's Close. Linton's sons were to found the successful Linton Bros butchers' shop at no 118. Until signage was erected in the 1970s closes had unofficial names usually indicating which shop they led to. Smith's Close had previously been known as Wyld's Close and Linton's Close. Smith was followed by Johnston the draper and by the late 1920s M and A Manson, ladies and children's outfitters occupied the shop followed by the Buttercup Dairy who moved from No 143 and Stewart Smith, Alex's son, electrician. Smith's Close was known as the Canongate Close before the twentieth century being a throughway between the High Street and the kirk. Beyond that is James Square, named after James Wyld. In the late 1800s it supported up to a dozen families, many in single rooms or attics. On entering the close there is a little door to the right which led to a room once used by Sam Landers, the horseshoe nailer and by Mr Polanska as a cobblers shop. The large stone just outside is said to have been used by Sam Landers as a seat while he made nails and many local posteriors have followed suit. The foot of the close had until quite recently its own 'gang'. This was in the form of a group of senior gentlemen who would pass their time chatting and putting the town and world to rights. The origins of the gang was as a meeting place for punters to place illicit bets with the bookie's runner in the days before Biggar had a legal betting office.

and linked up both upstairs and downstairs, an extra storey being put on the 1893 oil store for communication to the seed store made out of Hyslop's shed. Three buildings on the North Back Road were also part of the property, the middle one formerly the Govan Hall. Lambie's rig was sold to Brown Brothers in the 1920s for their factory and part of cemetery.

Nos 121 and 123. The Burgh Commissioners passed plans for John Vallance (1830-96) the saddler to build a new house and shop here in 1877. John's father James and grand-father William were also saddlers. The family history in Biggar went back to 1640. Mr Vallance had established a coach works with sliding doors on North Back Road in 1875. It was to become the original part of Gladstone Court Museum. No 123 was the business of Archibald Bogle, fishmonger, in 1901 and Annie Brown and family, butchers till 1920. It is on the site of an eighteenth century change-house (ale house or tavern) where J McGhie, farmer, of Moss-side was assaulted by his employee George Paterson. McGhie's son James took revenge by fatally felling Paterson with a pair of tongs. James was tried at Glasgow but having received a character witness from Lord Elphinstone, was given a particularly mild sentence – banishment from Scotland. He went to England but returned a few years later to become tenant of Langlees Farm and eventually emigrated to America.

Nos 125, 127 and 129, Masonic House. In 1845 the masonic brotherhood decided that the old house and inn on this site had rather too many leaks and proposed a new construction which was to be built in the same place for no more that £400. James Watt's plans (see No8) were accepted in 1846 and the new build completed in the late Georgian style. (The lodge behind dates from 1814). It incorporated the **Commercial Inn** whose keepers were William Kennedy in the 1840s till his death in 1851, James Frame in 1861, Roderick McKay in 1871 and 1881, William Gordon (who displayed a double duck egg from Inch of Howburn) in 1891 and John Galbraith in 1901. Kennedy's son, also William, left for Glasgow in 1853 and went on to found the Broxburn Oil Company, later to become part of British Petroleum. In 1880 McKay's wife, Agnes was discovered to have had an infidelity with her hostler, John Stewart. Stewart was sacked. The hotel consisted of a commercial room, parlour, six bedrooms, bar and conveniences. It suffered considerable fire damage in 1895 when high winds fanned flames from an attic room to James Wyld's property next door. The rear coach house, built in 1871 became Lambie's grate store. The front house was sold in 1958 to Mr Cairns for £1400. No 125 had been the Commercial Inn bar and became Biggar Town Council offices and an office for Smail and Ewart before moving to the National Bank building. The business at No 129 was also the property of the Masonic Lodge till 1953. In

Miss Gladstone had a thriving business and survived the 1931 fire. During the re-building she went to Miss Brown's Birch Cottage. She retired in 1958 in favour of her assistant Sheena Rae who moved down into the lower half of Central Tearooms. The upper part was connected into Miss Gladstone's old shop by a simple turn in the stair and a further opening added the shop to the premises (see 119).

The upstairs houses in the 1861 re-building were reached by an outside stair. A cast iron sink at the top of it served to remove most of the waste of various sorts. A Mrs Fruid stayed upstairs in No 113 in the 1920s. Jake Stewart and his wife, a sister of William Aitchison, carter came in 1931 but fire reduced their home before they were in residence though they lost some furniture. Mrs Stewart remained till about 1948, succeeded by Mrs Laura Dickson sister of Miss Gladstone (above) and Mrs Lambie, when she died suddenly there in July 1959. The shop foreman of 119, John Coupland, then moved up from No 30.

In 1861 the shop, 119, was occupied by Joseph Bertram, a grain merchant. He moved over to 116 in 1864 when 22 year old John Gladstone, Eastfield, Coulter began as an ironmonger. John was a brother of William Gladstone, draper and had served an apprenticeship with James Wyld the grocer. His first stock included bricks wrapped in paper. John bought the property from the Hunters in 1873 or thereabouts. His first office, described in Gilbert Rae's book *Langsyne in Braefoot*, Robert Gladstone was in the back shop. Later in 1893 he converted an oil cellar which lasted till 1962. He built a seed store in the 1880s and later Hyslop's store (1910) was taken over. He retired in 1900 and died in 1901. Rae, Gladstone and Brown, his successors split in 1906, Rae going to Victoria Buildings, Gladstone to Canada and D Brown, Gladstone's nephew continuing. Brown was the first to sell petroleum in Biggar and had a store near Brown's butchers' factory for 2 gallon cans. He died of dysentery returning from the Dardanelles in 1915. John Lambie from Glen Trool, who came as manager in 1913, became a partner with Brown's trustees and sole partner in 1919. In Nov 1931 the block suffered a major fire, believed to have been started by a fault in a recently installed electrical system. People who witnessed the start of the fire thought that guns were being shot but it was the sound of gun cartridges exploding in the fire. The office and store at the back were unaffected by the fire and functioned as a make-do shop. The front of the building was re-built to a design by Latto Morrison in 1932. The central upstairs window echoes the upper windows of the Royal Bank across the street. Shop windows had the coloured glazing along the tops removed for the 1971 street improvement scheme. Lambie bought it from John Gladstone's son, Sandy in 1946, the year Brian Lambie, his son, started with him. John died on the 31st of July 1963. In 1959 the shop extended and in 1962/3 the place was gutted

The fire-inflicted damage to Nos 113-119 in 1931.

lished some Biggar views. Later the Hunters' business declined and they sold the property to the three Gladstone brothers who later sold to one of their number, John, the tenant of No 119. John Brownlie was a grocer here in 1896 having taken over from David Hunter. Later Hyslop moved over from the Post Office Buildings. His landlords were the Auction Market Company and they wouldn't let him apply for a spirits license as they also had a hotel tenant at the Clydesdale Hotel. Hyslop had gone there in 1898 and later moved to No 63. After Hyslop the shop became a Ladies Fancy Repository, still retaining the tobacco license but not the spirit one, run by Jess Cranstoun. On her marriage in 1924 she sold out to her new sister-in-law, Susan B Gladstone, daughter of William Gladstone, draper (No 81-83).

Biggar Club, a group of emigrees who returned regularly to their native town to inspect good works and award prizes to school children. He built the Clydesdale Hotel in the 1870s and later moved to the temperance hotel at No 132. John Steele was there in 1915, Margaret McNicol in 1925 and Olive Corner ran the Crown in the 1930s and '40s making separate bar and lounge areas. Bruce Walker was the publican in the 1950s when one of his notable barmaids was Valda Grieve, wife of poet Hugh MacDiarmid. Jim White of Lanark re-instated the one-space bar in the 1980s and exposed the stone walls.

Nos 113-119. On a lintel re-built above a rear window are the initials PK.IW 1650. These were Patrick Kello, Bailie in Biggar and Janet Wast his wife, both of whom had wills registered in the 1680s. Patrick appears in an unfavourable light in Hogg's diary of 1659 where he was deposed from the session of the parish kirk. It is probably he who is referred to in the negotiation for the school/tollbooth also mentioned. The earliest titles refer to Bailie John Kello and thereafter the schoolmaster John Girdwood, (1730s) a prominent freemason. Simon Linton, merchant (buried at Broughton) was blind latterly and his trustees included his son-in-law Dr George Kello. Linton died c.1849 and the property was then occupied by William Hunter of Bathgate who re-built the block in 1861 using Carluke brick, which had by that time had become available via the railway, with a stone facing. The block became known as the 'Crystal Palace' as it was one of the first to use a plate glass frontage. The shop at 115 was occupied by John Mitchell (1870s) and Matthew Cuthbertson, draper, followed by Adam R Dickson, draper who was provost for several terms. After the 1914/18 war Dickson sold out as none of his family were to succeed and the shop became the Central Tearoom run by John D Brown (see No 88) son of James Brown, tailor and his two sisters Agnes and Meg Brown. After the latter's marriage, a younger sister, Liz came on board and for many years it was A and E Brown (without JD). They had a good home bakery and a busy tearoom. Agnes was a champion raffle ticket seller and first class gossip (The Hamilton Advertiser). All the family were musical to the benefit of the parish choir, Agnes singing soprano and Liz alto. They were excellent readers and able to sing or play a huge repertoire. Agnes often sang tenor when no men appeared and was responsible for nurturing many a youthful chorister who later captured her enthusiasm for things musical. The upstairs tearoom closed during the latter part of the war, re-opened and closed about 1955 though the shop continued. Agnes died in 1957 and Liz 1959 and the shop was divided up.

The middle shop, 117, was David Hunter's, after 1861. A son, Norman, was a photographer at Port Glasgow and pub-

expression in Biggar for many years after. John Archibald, later owned by William Lithgow, grocer was at 107 from at least 1868 to the 1880s. Archibald employed six men and three boys in 1871. The Greenshields and Lithgow partnership (David Greenshields had been the manager in 1901 after Archibald's death in 1891 and William Lithgow worked for Archibald) had the business from 1902 to be succeeded by R & J Brownlie in 1949. Robert Brownlie died in 1972. He claimed on his letter heading that the Greenshield and Lithgow business had been established in 1755. This presumably refers to a business earlier than Wyld's on the same site. Lt Col John Cobb of the US Air Force took over in 1973. The room to the left was the office of Neil Black the carrier in the early twentieth century which became Young's Express Deliveries before nationalisation in 1948.

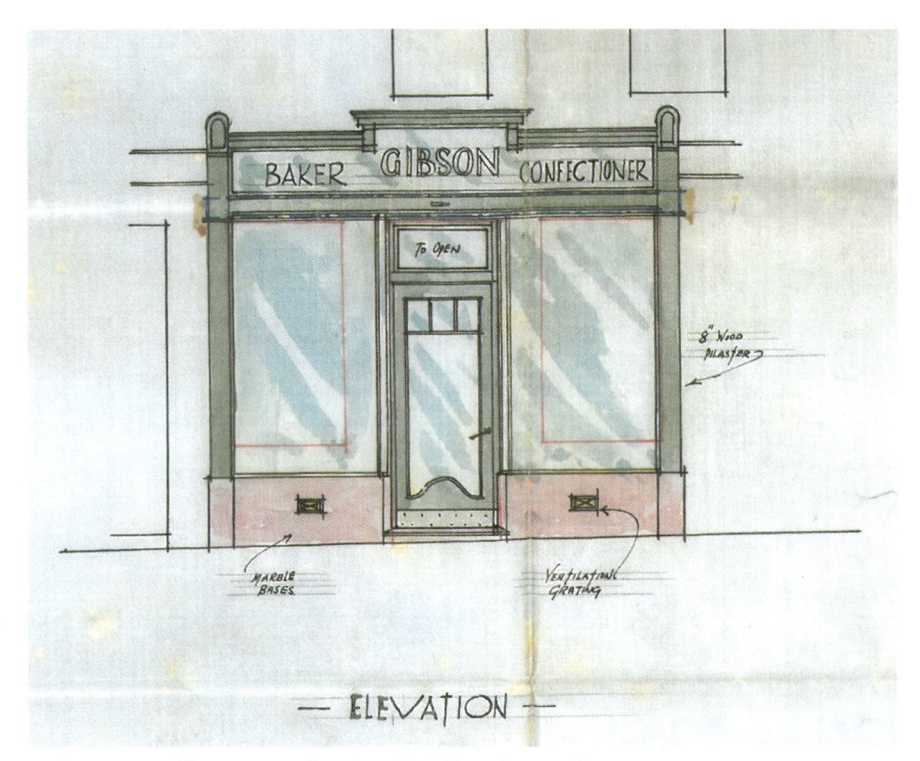

The 1928 Duff St Joinery drawing for Gibson's new frontage.

At **Nos 109-111 the Crown Inn** dates from the late 18th century, possibly as late as 1820. In 1858 it was listed as a two-storey slated house in good repair, the property of Mrs Craig. A porch with bathroom above was added in the rear angle of the building in 1896 along with a urinal in the corner of the building opposite the porch. The building was altered around 1900 with double front doors added but reverted back to a single door in the 1980s. William Craig owned the hotel in 1865 followed by David Thomson by 1875 and from the 1840s to '70s Walter Toward from Pettinain was the publican with Robert Russell from the 1880s. Toward was renowned for his purveying being the regular host of the Edinburgh

Gibson's new fleet of baker's vans in the 1950s. They were painted red and brown with gold lettering.

cupied by Adam Foggart, printer in 1868 followed by William Alcock, chief magistrate on the burgh council, in the 1880s, James Jackson in the 1890s and Thomas Gibson. It became part of Fred Stephen's car showroom in the twentieth century. Jackson the stationer started there in 1908 to be succeeded by his son who retired in 1958 and followed for a short time by WP Bryden. **No 93** was for over 100 years a butcher's shop. Walter Scott was there in the 1880s followed by David Halliday and Robert Russell of the Crown Hotel in 1884, then the Brown family, John from 1920. The Browns' business functioned in Biggar from 1885 at a now demolished building on the corner of Station Road where James W Brown, born in Crawford in 1857, arrived in Biggar via Peeblesshire. James died in the 1890s to be followed by his son, Archibald and his sons till the 1980s. It was latterly taken over by the Biggar Auction Market Company but the name lives on in Brown Brothers cooked meats. Standing just inside the door was a large stookie pig, about three feet high, dressed in a striped butchers apron holding its hoofed arm out with a square platter and always a great source of amusement. The adjoining Gibson's Close was home to Gavin and Stewart's electrical business in the 1950s.

Prior to the erection of the present building **No 99** hosted John Graham, baker from 1793 and Walter Rae, shoemaker in the 1880s. The present frontage was designed in 1928 by the Duff St Joinery in Edinburgh for AJ Gibson who had moved from Innerleithen in 1913. His sons William and Thomson took over in the 1950s and expanded the business with a new bakehouse and fleet of vans. Gibson's Close to the west was the site of James Adams's barber's shop.

At **101**, George Wilson, baker was a contemporary of Graham and Rae. He had a bakehouse to the rear which was the site of a tragic fire in the 1880s when adjacent stables were burned and several horses perished. WP Bryden had a stationer's shop here before the Second World War before moving to No 153. In 1946 Gibson next door converted the shop to the art nouveau styled Thistle Tea Rooms and continues to function as a restaurant.

The prominent building with Doric columns, entablature and balustrade at **Nos 105 and 107** dating from the late 18th century became the Western Bank. From its opening in 1839 it was managed in turn by Messrs Wyld, Jackson and Thomson till suspension in 1857 under similar circumstances to the City of Glasgow Bank. Two Wyld brothers ran the grocery business next door at 107. The elder brother was patronised by a town worthy who ingratiated himself with Wyld to the extent of cadging a daily dram, free gratis. When Wyld the younger took over from his brother the worthy expected the same hospitality but was met with the line 'Nothing for nothing in my shop!' It became a household

17th July 1907 – the procession preceding the opening of the new public park.

A conjectural sketch by Brian Lambie of the old UP manse on the site of Nos 89-95. The old UP church gable can be seen beyond. Evidence of the Post Office at No 87 is disputed.

garages between 1979 and 1981. Stephens maintained the Biggar ambulance fleet in the 1950s and '60s.

Nos 89 to 95 (Linton's Buildings) occupy the site of the old United Presbyterian manse. The UP church was behind the manse (still exists as a residential development) before relocating to the Moat Park. The manse was described in 1858 as a plain two storey dwelling. It was demolished and converted to shops and houses in 1865 but the Burgh Commissioner's Records stated that the 'Regular slope of pavement to be preserved on demolition'. The UP church (later Moat Park) minister was the Rev John Low for 43 yrs. He was a pious man but had a nasty temper. In 1780, his son, who at the time was a divinity student, was accused of fathering an illegitimate child which he denied. The baby's mother could not afford to care for the child and she asked for parochial assistance from the established church (St Mary's), whose minister, Rev William Watson and his elders, summoned young Low to explain why he would not support his ascribed child. Low refused to attend an established church hearing and when a further summons was delivered by Robert Forsyth, the church officer, Rev Low Senior gave Forsyth an ear-bashing, kicked his nether regions and thrust him into the street. The Rev Low was charged with assault but the justices considered it trivial and did not inflict a penalty, much to the annoyance of many of the large audience who had assembled to see the minister humbled. **No 89** was oc-

The National Bank at No 79, Adam Pairman, draper at 81, James Stephen, plumber and tinsmith at 85, William Alcock, printer at 89, Walter Scott, butcher at 93, James graham, baker at 97, Walter Rae, shoemaker at 99, George Wilson, baker at 101, former Western Bank at 105, John Archibald, grocer at 107, Crown Inn at 109 etc. C.1880.

five months trading in Biggar. Following a series of dodgy investments and prospectuses its directors, including Robert Stronach, were jailed as a result of their deceit. Walter Smith wrote – "Rotten from rind to the core, From beginning to end, Wrong all my life heretofore, And now it won't mend, And there is the wolf at its door!"

It was taken over by the National Bank. Adam Pairman, its agent (he was offered the post on the recommendation of his brother Robert, the surgeon, who had declined the offer) was the founder of a drapery business on the site and continued to act as agent for the National Bank next door. He retired in April 1882 and was succeeded by his son William Brown Pairman then by his assistants with the store becoming the iconic Gladstone and Core. William Gladstone, grand-father of Brian Lambie, from Eastfield was the older brother of John Gladstone who was to run the ironmongery at No 119. His partner, Tom Core, was a manger of the Moat Park Kirk and its session clerk for many years. Core attended to the business while Gladstone toured the Tweed Valley with his pony and trap to take orders from customers. Core was some twenty years younger than Gladstone and when he died the business was bought by John Millar then DC McNaught of Coatbridge. Jimmy Cowan and Jessie Eastland went into partnership from 1957 until Jessie's retirement in 2017.

Nos 85-87 sit on the site of an old tenement which belonged to a Dr Bertram d.1815, aged 63. It was occupied by Mr Hamilton, a druggist and horse doctor, the subject of satirical writing by James Affleck who noted the maltreatment of Hamilton's own horse. Another occupant was William Sim who lived there from 1814 till his death in 1825. His house was disordered and dirty but contained a large collection of books. He used the contents of these books to discourse with his contacts to the point of boredom in what would be described today as pseudo-intellectual drivel. People tried hard to avoid him. He had acquired a job as school master in Quothquan and kept a diary of his time there in the late 1790s which he used to write an autobiography. He also wrote of his loves – Miss Kello of Skirling Mill who rejected him and had her servants see him on his way with banter and ridicule, Miss Brown of Edmonston, Miss Davidson of Coats and Jess Walker of Peeblesshire. All these unrequited loves seem to have caused him great mental anguish. He suffered a stroke in 1820 which rendered him partially lame and spent the last of his days relying on neighbourly and parochial charity. Later, up to 1864, Matthew Robertson, watchmaker was there but he moved to No 94 (Hislop's old place). James Stephen, the tinsmith (or whitesmith – a worker in light metals) and plumber occupied the present building in the 1880s. It became Fred Stephen's garage in the twentieth century, still under the name of James Stephen until Sherwood Skelly arrived and rationalised three Biggar

Across the street c.1880.

form of architecture. A date stone of 1863 sits above the eastern door and above that, in a vesics piscis (oval recess), St Andrew. The architect was Alexander Fraser of Dumfries and the builder was Ebeneezer McMorran. It functioned as the bank and bank house. The bank closed in the 1970s and the upper portion was then used as the Burgh Council Chambers. The area in front of the building was the site of Biggar's first vintage car rally in 1971 before moving to Hope's Rigg and the Showfield.

The City of Glasgow Bank was next door to the National Bank at **Nos 81 and 83**. It was suspended in 1857 after only

No 63 - Proctor and Weir's c.1900.

sweet and toy shop and was renovated by Miss Pagan in the 1940s. No 12 was the home of Jimmy Jamieson the photographer and the house next to Biggar Kirk, No 14, was the beadle's house built in the 1870s and raised to a second storey in the 1950s when it was renamed Kilmeny after the buyers, Miss Johnston and Miss Gentles swapped their so named house in Broughton Road with the Kirk Session. Before the churchyard was expanded in the 1870s there were two more small houses on Kirkstyle and the remains of the walls of one of these houses can still be seen behind the Wilson and Johnston family graves.

No 63 was the business of Proctor and Weir, plumbers and later RB Marr's, Tucker's and Adamson's grocery store. Marr used the upper floor of the old school house on Kirkstyle as his granary. Weir from Torphichen was to break away from Proctor in 1909 to form his own business at No 136. **No 67** was Ramsay's cooperage in the early 1800s until Ramsay became Biggar's first gas maker in 1840. It then housed Thomas Mitchell, saddler from around 1900 (his son William was killed in Egypt in 1915). Another son, George, took over and passed it on to his assistant Bobby Smith. It later became Jenny Wren's art store. At **No 69** the existing sign covers a cut out lettered 'Jeweller & Watchmaker' sign erected in 1903 by John G Brown with a distinctive art nouveau style. This shop would, in the early part of the 1900s, display the largest Cairngorm stone in the world in its window. It later became Yuill's jewellery shop.

No 73 Birch Cottage. This was the home of John Brown the fiddler. Johnny liked a drink. Once, returning from Broughton after a gig he had to sit down feeling extremely sick and fearing his time was up. However he got himself together and said to himself "If I maun dee, I may as well dee gaun as sittin' ", and he eventually got himself home. Plans were passed in January 1876 for the present Birch Cottage to be built by Thomas Brown and in 1903 for the adjoining watchmaker's shop, **No 71**. The communicating door with No 71 was built up in 1963 when JG Brown retired.

No 75, Davaar, is the old Biggar Kirk manse. It was built in 1805 with 1827, 1840 and 1880 additions. It ceased to be the manse in the 1880s when the Rev Duncan found it too primitive for his family to live in, a new manse being built on Carwood Road and Davaar became a boarding house. It was later bought by Dr Archibald Campbell and had become the home of Alex Weir, plumber and family by 1901. A Victorian era well was discovered in 2016 during preparations for a new western extension. The well has since been filled in and capped.

Built as the National Bank in 1863 on the site of two previous buildings one of which was a pub and the other a house occupied by Adam and Agnes Pairman, **Nos 77 and 79** was described by Hunter as having, for Biggar, an advanced

The renovation of Kirkstyle houses in 1971.

the residents here was Menzies Moffat the tailor and photographer who sewed the magnificent and monumental Royal Centre Crimean War Hero Table Cover and the Star or Transforming Table Cover which are displayed in the Biggar and Upper Clydesdale Museum. Moffat's work was celebrated throughout North America where in 1888 many newspapers reported his skills and hoped for a North American tour. Miss Hastie, the dressmaker was there in 1897. Next door at No 6, Saughtrees, is the site of the 1860s Post Office in a whinstone and thatch building run by Alan Whitfield, father of Aaron Whitfield. Alan was a friend of William Hunter and assisted him with research for 'Biggar and the House of Fleming'. It was rebuilt in sandstone in the 1870s and became James Stirling's boot and shoe maker's business and there is still a very feint remnant of his sign on the front of the building. It then became Miss Adams's

Robert (Burnie) Lithgow and William Carruthers, bootmaker and cobbler, Kirkstyle c.1890.

John Aitchison plying his craft at the School Green smiddy in 1953.

Morrison to Mr Wilson, the joiner in 1881. The space to the east of the old schoolhouse was the site of a water tank, the first attempt to provide a piped water supply for Biggar using a pipe from Hillhead. The flow was too slow and replaced eventually by the King's Beck supply.

A memorial to Dr John Brown, born in Biggar in 1810 was mounted on the south wall of the Municipal Hall in 1923 after a public subscription was led by Gilbert Rae. Dr Brown practiced in Edinburgh and was the author of, amongst other works, 'Rab and his Friends'. Another memorial sits in front. This is to James Cuthbertson and is in the form of a snow-plough. His engineering works is still a major employer in the town and his gritters and snow ploughs help keep our roads safe in winter. Cuthbertson's bespoke drainage and ploughing machines have been exported to six continents.

The street name '**Kirkstyle**' only appears from 1881; before that census addresses included the street as part of the 'North Side of Street'. The single-storey houses on the eastern side of Kirkstyle were re-built c.1971. Only the front façade is original. Amongst

hear the groans of the poor sinners being tortured by the devil!

> *The great storm of February 1884 was also responsible for great damage to the roofs and windows of the Commercial and Elphinstone Hotels as well as the properties of Messrs Rae, Stronach, Kello and Archibald. Slates, chimney cans and rhones littered the High Street and a 23cwt piece of lead was carried 60 yards beyond the roof of Carwood House.*

The **Moat Park Church** was built in 1865 to a Lombardic Romanesque design by Peddie and Kinnear. It replaced the building behind No 91 High St and functioned until 1978. It was bought by the Biggar Museum Trust and became their flagship Heritage Centre from 1988 until 2015 and has since become a residential building.

The name, School Green, comes from its association with the Burgh or West Public School which occupied the Municipal Hall site. In 1767 William Law mortified (left in his will) £41 and in 1817 William Nisbet mortified £40, the interest of both sums to be applied in educating poor children. The education consisted of classes in English, writing, arithmetic, geography, Greek, Latin, French and mathematics. The attendance was 180 but other private schools including the South School on South Back Road and the East Industrial School on Mid Road attracted more pupils. The original burgh school was re-built in 1798 and extended in 1830 at a cost of £600 but deemed unsatisfactory by the Rev John Christison who proposed a new build in 1849. The work designated by the Church Parochial Board (which had responsibility for public education before the 1872 Education Act) was completed by 1860 under the contract of Clarke and Bell. It was one large partitioned room with teacher's room to the side and had leaded windows. As the Corse Knowe had been removed by this time the pupils of the burgh school revived the 'hurley hacket' as the 'mushy mell' down the slope at the front of the building in snowy winters. When the new High School was built in 1901 the old school became the **Municipal Hall** designed by JL Murray who adapted the building in the Jacobean style. It also functioned as the burgh court for the trying of minor offences. The toilet block on the western at side is by LA Morrison. An addition of 1958 by JJ Shannon included the barrel vaulted council chamber upstairs opened by Miss Elizabeth Mitchell. The council moved to more spacious premises in the National Bank building in the 1960s till the end of the council in 1975. The house opposite the school, now No 9 Kirkstyle, was the old school built in 1798 and became the teachers' house, a somewhat larger property that would have been the norm as teachers were expected to take in lodgers, until a new school house was built on Viewpark Road. The house was sold by James

School Green (Kirkstyle). The properties along the western side of the School Green, at one time marking the western extent of the High Street proper, belonged to Robert Lithgow, Hislop and the Cree family recorded on a feu of 1836 when Biggar Estate was broken up and Carwood Estate took over this land.

No 1, School Green Cottage, was the home of Alexander Tait of Haldane and Tait, Motor Engineers of South Back Road.

No 5 was Lawrence Hislop the blacksmith's house dating to the 1830s. A marriage lintel of 1842 sits above the door. When Lawrence ceased work (he died in 1888) his daughter, Miss Hislop established a school for girls in the house till around 1909. She was a Master of Arts, Biggar's first female graduate. The school, which was favoured for the daughters of many local farmers, later relocated to Dunreath (Hillcrest) on Coulter Rd. John Aitchison re-established the blacksmith business next door at **No 3** in 1903 with four recesses for new forges. Aitchison's work can be seen in the railings around the war memorial and other buildings but much was lost in the government's 1942 salvage drive when gates and railings were collected throughout the country for munitions. Brian Lambie recalled, when working in his father's ironmonger's shop, being sent to Aitchison to have tools repaired or sharpened and ruining more than one pair of boots by standing on red-hot fragments from the hearth. He was succeeded by Jack Angus of Thankerton, the Angus family living there from 1959 to 2001.

There was a row of Carwood Estate cottages in front of the site of the municipal hall in the early 1800s occupied by the Cree and Beaumont families and demolished in 1849. Matthew Cree was born in 1742 and was Biggar's Baron Bailie for 27 years. He was noted for his ability to solve legal problems informally advising aggrieved parties to "Tak a gill an' 'gree". He was a wealthy man and was liable for Land tax of £21-7/9d. on his properties at Stanehead on Broughton Road and east of the Camb. His son, Gavin (1782-1860) gained excellence as a seedsman and tree pruner. In 1848 he won the London Society of Arts Gold Medal for pruning methods involving the foreshortening of branches. His skills had him working in The Meadows and Princes St Gardens in Edinburgh. The Crees' nursery at Moat Park (before the church was built) was surrounded by beech trees which they had planted in the 1750s. The trees on Kirkstyle blew down in a storm in February 1884* but one original tree still stands on the Burn Braes. An attempt was made by the Biggar Museum Trust to replicate the Crees' trees by planting memorial beeches to their long-term volunteers in the grounds of the Heritage Centre. An older tree, cut down by the Crees, was known as the deil's tree as the devil was thought to inhabit its upper branches. Put your ears to the trunk and you could

Gala day procession 1908 passes Nos 47-59. The Jacobean Inn on the left and George Duncan, tailor beyond.

The 'Great Flood' of 2nd August 1915 outside No 45, Elphinstone Cottage. Gilbert Rae claimed to have made a snowball with the accompanying hail.

No 53, Cosy Neuk was Paterson's china warehouse and carter's stable below in the nineteenth century. A sign for the china business, which had been used as a worktop, was discovered to have been overwritten on a sign for James Cairns, Mrs Paterson's father.

Built in 1883, **No 55** was the home and shop of James Tweedie and George Duncan, tailors from October 1890. George Wilson was a painter there in the 1950s, taken over by Ian Findlay in 1960. G Tarr's antique business was there in the 1970s. **No 57** was William Minto (1847-1914), the coal merchant's.

No 61, the former Moat Park Manse was built to a JL Murray design in 1881 and had been the site of Biggar's bowling green from 1848 till the 1870s. When a new garage was built in the 1950s for the Rev Warnock a 10ft cube subterranean water tank was discovered and swallowed up one of Cuthbertson's machines.

Beside the flagpole at the junction with Kirkstyle sits a sundial sculpted by Ian Hamilton Finlay in 1970 to mark European Conservation Year. It was originally placed in front of the Corn Exchange to mark the inauguration of the Biggar townscape conservation scheme.

you very much" Kowalski and others, had taken over the delicatessen business at No 33.

Nos 37 and 39 are built onto No 35 and of the same style but a few years later (1877). There are attic windows otherwise they are identical with the adjoining block. No 39 hosted M Douglas and the Mauchline Boot and Shoe Company after Messrs Shiels moved over the street to larger premises. During the war it was empty and Mr Cumming of Biggar Park, later Coulter Mains, displayed his large model of the Queen Mary in its window in aid of the Red Cross. Aitken and McLean, painters took it after the war with Mrs McLean selling pictures and a little china. Aitken left to trade on his own and Tom McLean eventually died about 1955. Mrs Petrie, then Tommy O' Donnell, had the premises in the late 20th century.

No 43 is another James Watt building and John Ballantine (1812-80), shoemaker 's sign is still visible above and beside the door.

No 45, Elphinstone Cottage. A mid-19th century house with large dormers sympathetically added in 1913 by LA Morrison. It was named by Miss Middleton of the Elphinstone Hotel who retired there after 1865. It became the home and office of JJ Shannon, architect in the post-war years. Wraggle marks on the stonework of Nos 43 and 47 indicate that a building or buildings once occupied the front garden space of the cottage.

No 47. This is probably the oldest building facing the present line of the High Street. It was built in the late 17th or early 18th century having two storeys of rubble with ashlar dressings, a slate roof and four-window front. The central chimney gablet has a single light window. Stone skews line the roof with scroll skew putts. It was once owned by the Vallance family, subsequently James and William Paterson. It was one of Biggar's chief eighteenth century inns and housed some officers of the Highland Army in 1745. They employed James Ramage to distribute letters to local proprietors and farmers demanding provisions. The Highlanders rewarded Ramage on his return with a glass of brandy and asked him to drink to the health of Prince Charles (Charles Edward Stuart, Bonnie Prince Charlie). "Na, na" , replied James, "I'll drink neither Prince Charles's health nor King Geordie's, but I'll joost drink yer ain." Young William Vallance, eight at that time, was given the job, with his friends, of relocating his father's horses from Boghall Mains to the Tweeddale hills to prevent them being requisitioned by the Highlanders. It became known as the Jacobean Inn. Marrion Lauder had it as a toyshop in the 1880s and in 1908 the building is seen to be harled and was a grocer's business. The low front door is an indication of the rise in the level of the pavement and road, not the height of its inhabitants. When it was built it would have been the westernmost building on the High Street.

The four houses on **Mitchell Knowe** were built at the bequest of land donor Elizabeth Mitchell for widows or single women. Elizabeth, whose grand-father had built Langlees in 1890, was Scotland's first female town planner and served on the East Kilbride Development Corporation. In an article in the Hamilton Advertiser of 1948 she described Biggar High Street as 'the finest street in the country'.

31, 33 and 35 Hislop's Buildings. This block was built by an old Biggar family, the Hislops, who were originally blacksmiths at the Schoolgreen on Kirkstyle. The block was built in 1860 and this date was worked into the slates at the back and the initials JH on the front. The shop, 33, and a workshop erected at the back in the early 1900s were occupied by Robert Hislop, tailor and later his son till 1951. Robert was the last treasurer of the Whipmen Society (a celebration of horsemanship) from 1806 to 1883 and in the shop were kept the box, minute books and flag now in the Biggar and Upper Clydesdale Museum. John Hislop stayed at Glenholm in Blawhill Road and was the last working master tailor in Biggar. At one time in the shop was the last hat ordered by the Rev John Christison DD who died before he could collect it. It was an enormous light coloured low top hat and as nobody else had a head big enough to fit it, it was regarded as a curiosity. After John Hislop's retiral the shop and workshop were used from 1955 by John Ramsay, cabinetmaker formerly with Moffat and Weir of Park Place. The workroom at the back was built in 1907.

The house upstairs, No 31, was occupied in the 1970s by Aggie Inch, Mrs Hugh Hamilton. She lit the bonfire in the '80s and died soon after. It was later owned by Sheila Scott who transcribed many of the monumental inscriptions in Upper Ward graveyards and ran the John Buchan centre in Broughton for many years. She harled the gable-end of the building and removed the back sheds.

No 35 was Miss Roberta Mc Guffie's ladies and children's outfitters which was stacked to the roof with stock. Everything was taken out of parcels to be shown and carefully put back in its place before the next item could be examined. The original tenant was George Mitchell, watchmaker before he crossed the street in 1909. A feature in his window in the 1890s was a clock with a sort of acrobatic movement on top which fascinated the young JG Brown who bought it at a sale about 60 years later and restored it. He was followed by Andrew Selkirk, saddler and a location for the West End Dairy in the 1930s. After Miss McGuffie, it became Zilla Reid's arts and crafts studio and Rudolph Ciplok's Continental Photographic Studio then an accountant's office, first as Peted Business Services (the Ed being Miss McGuffie's nephew, Edmund Pretswell, grocer), then JA Fleming of Symington. It was finally incorporated into the Laird's Larder after Charles Thorpe Junior, successor to Fred "thank

This image taken at West End around 1863 is one of the earliest photographic records of the High Street. It features Walter Brunton, the butcher, and Agnes Crawford (carrying the baby) later Mrs John Rae, mother of Gilbert Rae, ironmonger and poet. To her right are the Bruntons' twin sons.

en's had a very futuristic sign in the style of Fritz Lang's Metropolis designed by DG Millar. The Campbell family ran three businesses in the Victoria Buildings in the '50s and the site became known as Campbell's Row. Allan Campbell was born in Lanark in 1875 and died at No 19 in 1954. His sons, Ed and Allan continued the business.

No 15 was the site of Gilbert Rae's ironmonger's business up to the early '60s. The Rae family is still prominent in Biggar. Gilbert was born in 1875 and apprenticed to John Gladstone at No 119. He died in 1955 having been succeeded by his son, John and run for a short time from 1970 by Brian Lambie. Rae became an accomplished poet and the town thought him worthy enough to have a housing development off the North Back Road named after him. He was largely responsible for saving the last of the ruins of Boghall Castle. A corrugated iron shed behind the buildings was Gilbert Rae's store.

The building to the east of Victoria Buildings, **Nos 17-21**, Victoria Place, was built in 1886 as the Post Office and telegraph office replacing the unit on John Street. The move was unannounced and took many people by surprise. Brunton the butcher, who later moved to No 116, was there in a previous building. John Graham the butcher was there from 1899 taking over from William Semple and followed by the Campbells before being taken over by the Hamiltons when Campbell retired in 1986. The Hamilton's store, No 21, was the Post Office before moving to its prominent site at No 80. An ornate mason's stone above the entrance reads 'B & J W'.

Between Nos 23 and 25 is the entrance to Moat Cottages built in the 1880s.

No25 was the business of John Black, the grocer then William Low the draper in the 1880s followed by Main of Carnwath's fruit and veg. C May's shoe shop was there in the 1970s.

Nos 27-29. James Wilson, baker occupied this site from the 1880s under the management of John Wilson. The business was established in 1842 but probably not on this site. In 1903 the back house was enlarged by taking down a dividing wall and since then the loft above has been removed. The tearoom, hayloft, van houses, stables etc. were all built then and the house, previously entered through the shop, was given a front door and porch at the expense of a bedroom or parlour. A hall was also built which was let out for dances and wedding receptions. The last Wilson brothers were Tom and George whose widows continued to run the business from the 1950s. It was taken over by David Bell of Shotts till 1973 and several minor alterations were carried out. The door from the shop to the house was blocked up and a passage formed straight through to the bake-house. The old parlour on the front street was a tearoom for some time in the 1950s and the Young Farmers' Club committees once met there.

Neilson Bridge and Victoria Buildings in the 1920s. Note the futuristic signage above Niven's stores.

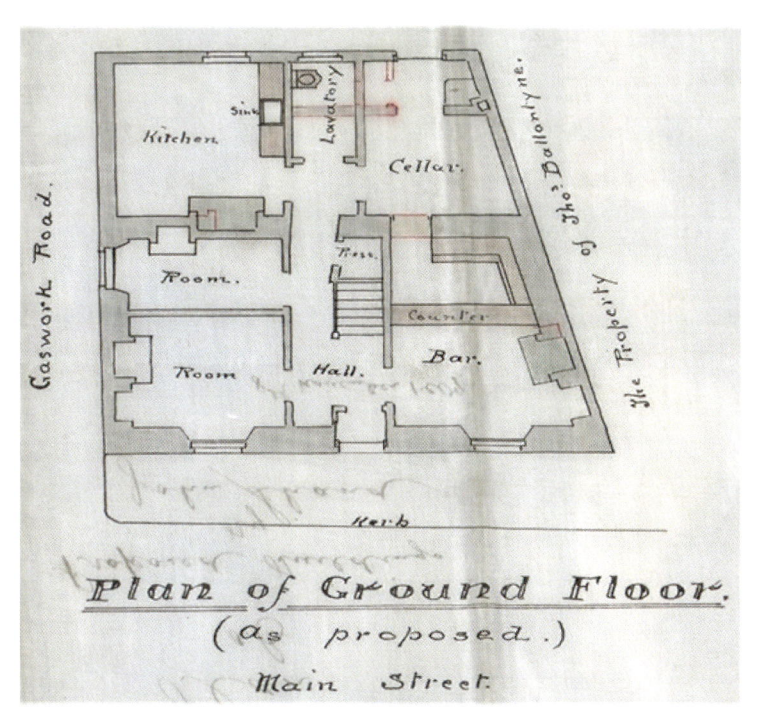

Thomas Garlaw's plan for alterations to the Cross Keys in 1909 for John Shand.

beds. John Shand had taken over ownership and management by 1915 and it became known as Shand's Hotel. James MacGregor had the establishment in the 1940s and the Butlers in the '50s. In 1951 the Biggar Burn burst its banks after a storm and snow melt which resulted in the ground floor of the Cross Keys and other nearby properties inundated with flood water. Furniture was ruined and stocks of beer, wine and spirits lost including three barrels of beer which floated down the burn towards Broughton.

The Victoria Buildings encompass **Nos 3, 5, 7, 9, 11 and 15**. In the nineteenth century this site was filled with a row of single and two-storey buildings including in 1880 a branch of Robert Hall of Lockerbie, boot and shoe merchants and run by J Crawford. Plans were drawn up in October 1905 for James Ballantyne (prompting the term Ballantyne's Buildings as an early alternative to the official name) by Architect William Brown Jnr. of Paisley. It is Biggar's only three-storey tenement building whose shops below are high ceilinged featuring cast-iron pillars to support the upper flats. The block has a roughcast front with Dumfriesshire sandstone facings and originally had communal toilets on each landing.

Nos 3 and 5 are now part of the Cross Keys but had various occupants throughout the twentieth century. Nelson's Westfield Dairy was there in 1910 followed by the milliner and ladies outfitter, Margaret Roberts. Tweeddale Electrics followed in the 1930s and Campbell's Dairy and Mary Campbell's hairdressers in the 1950s.

Nos 7 and 9 have hosted S Kelly, fishmonger and poulterer in the early 1900s, A Ewing and J&C Niven, outfitters in the mid-war years, 1948 James H. Brownlie, hairdresser in the 1940s and William P Campbell, outfitters in the '50s. Niv-

Robert Johnstone, drapers in 1867. Robert Linn the grocer moved there from No 7 in 1899. Moffat and Weir, cabinet-makers occupied the building in the twentieth century and later Mrs Fairbairn had her Tartan Teashop there followed by the Scottish Mill Shop. Moffat and Weir made much of their own good quality furniture at a factory in Station Road. John Weir was Biggar's provost in the 1930s. James Woodhouse and Son of Edinburgh opened a branch of their furniture business there in 1960. The building has been the home to a Chinese restaurant for the past forty years.

The house on the site of **No 5** was occupied in the 1920s and '30s by Mrs Oliver who ran a chip shop from her home, the front window being always open for customers, many who came from the West Row to buy chips which she would make to order.

No 7 is shown as a public house on the OS 1st edition map of 1857. It was the location of Robert Linn's and William Inglis' grocery businesses from the 1870s, taken over by T Renwick in 1920 and James C Bonsor by 1930. Inglis died aged 31 in 1876 but the business was continued by his widow, Annie. (The building was owned by Jemima Hederrwick in 1895 but had been bought by Anne Inglis before her death in 1906). The building was demolished around 1938 for a purpose-built fish shop with a glass fascia. This is a distinctive building with moulded cement detail on the corner. The modern upvc windows sympathetically follow the Lanarkshire vernacular lying panes, originally in cast iron frames. The 1950s housing unit to the left replaced a lower roof-line. The public weigh-bridge was located on Park Place in 1885.

Next to the burn is the War Memorial, revealed in 1920 by Walter Elliot MP. It was designed by David G Millar (1877-1925) in the style of Biggar's old merkat cross. Millar's work cost £1335, raised by public subscription and the land donated by the Trust Estate of David Black but not before a protracted squabble over the boundaries of the land especially on the west side of the burn which up till then housed the coal boxes of the houses on Park Place. Millar also designed the High School memorial and one for Elsrickle Church. The World War II inscriptions were added later. A few metres upstream is **Wallace Cottage**, so named because of the William Wallace story, and home to Mrs Brunton's millinery business for a short while from 1902 before moving to No 64. Isabella Wybar ran her dressmaker's business from here in 1911.

Back to the High Street proper …

No 1 – The Cross Keys was run by Catherine Mitchell (1880) who was licensed to retail spirits, porter and ale and around 1900 by her daughter, Mrs Lamb. The hotel featured in Joseph Laing Waugh's 'Robbie Doo' in 1912 on a journey from Thornhill to Edinburgh. Robbie disliked the bugs in the

William Inglis's store at No 7 Park Place c.1905, replaced in 1938. R – Mina Inglis and L - Auntie Big Mag.

Planting the burgh quincentenary trees at Townhead in 1951.

fought in the Boer War (1899-1902). He was an expert plasterer who spent some of his life in North America where he had indulged in some contraband across the Canadian/American border thus the name 'smuggler'. He joined the Canadian Black Watch pipe band during the First World War. Smug died in 1957.

George Wilson built the houses in the eponymous **George Square** in the 1860s. **No 162** was his house and later the home of John Dickson the nurseryman and has a fine moulded stone surround to the back door.

No 168 was the home of John and Margaret Pretswell whose son John was Biggar's first casualty of the First World War. A plaque in front of the house commemorates the planting of cherry trees around George Square in 1951 to mark Biggar's quincentenary. One tree was planted by 101 year-old Gavin Allan, a retired joiner who had worked on the Kirk restoration of 1870. The trees surround a small seated area which is the home to Biggar's poetry garden. Established in 2000 for the Biggar Millennium Project by South Lanarkshire Council, some twenty poetical works from fourteen of Scotland's leading writers including Burns, MacDiarmid and MacCaig are represented by short engraved extracts of their works.

Behind **No 170** was the Langvout, where houses with long vaults once stood. One of the keystones of the vaulted houses was carved with the Lockhart arms. On demolition, Adam Sim of Coulter acquired the stone and presented it to William Lockhart who mounted it in the hall of Milton Lockhart House. As Milton Lockhart was dismantled in 1987 and rebuilt in Japan, there may be a small part of Biggar amusing visitors in a Japanese theme park. One of the houses, described as a wretched hovel, acted as the town prison confining many drunk beggars, the lunatic who set fire to nannie Muir's house and the tinker who felled his companion at the Ba' Green. Another was the lodging house of Samuel Bell. In 1747 Bell and his wife Agnes Noble were brought before the bailie, Robert Leckie, having had complaints from their neighbours about allowing 'vagrants, tinkers, sorners and sturdy beggars' to reside in their house. They were banished to West Linton for two months!

No 170 sits on the site of a store built for Andrew Lawson the fruiterer to garage his lorry. Upstairs, in the 1940s, was the workshop of Stevenson and Short, cabinet makers and Biggar's camera club met there for a time.

No 172, Stane Cottage, was once the home of Menzies Pairman the roadman. The plasterer's business of T Glaister was run from here in the 1910s. It was bought by Andrew Lawson (see above) in the early 1930s.

Fearnville, **No 174** and the joiners' workshop behind were built for Hugh Ross in March 1903. The house once contained a sideboard and mantelpiece of oak from the parish

Sillerknowe and George Square c.1880. Andrew Black's smiddy the first single storey building from the right and on the extreme left the gable end of what is possibly Biggar's oldest building.

panded over next ten years allowing him to employ ten men and one boy. He provided accommodation for two blacksmith journeymen, James Black and Thomas Christie as well as John Noble, a master mason, James and George Porteous, (father and son) cattle dealers and James Porteous, a grocer. The smithy was later taken over by Alex Weir (no relation to Weir the plumber) in the 1870s and transferred to John Brown in 1900 before becoming Walter B Stephen's garage and most recently the home of the amalgamated Biggar and Upper Clydesdale Museum. Stephen was the son of James Stephen the plumber at No 85 and started in the plumber's yard but split with his father to form his own motor business at Townhead. Walter installed his first petrol pump at the kerb side in 1924. The name of the business confusingly changed to James Stephen and Sons when Sherwood Skelly bought and rationalised the Central, Jubilee and Townhead Garages on the Townhead site around 1980. A marriage stone – ID : EM 1671 – above the door to No 158 relates to the Dalziel family.

No 160 was the home of Smug (smuggler) Smith who had

by William Bogle, a carter. George Bertram, a smith, was in 148 at the same time.

The area around **Nos 150, 152 and 154** has been greatly altered in the last forty years. It is the site of the **Siller Knowe** which witnessed business transactions before banks were established in the town. The buildings here were the property of Andrew Brown and family in the early eighteenth century. His son Richard was a weaver and he had several children with his wife, Tibbie Forrest including John, an excise man and Andrew, born 1763, who became a distinguished minister. He emigrated to Halifax, Nova Scotia in 1787 to take charge of the Scots Kirk there. He returned in 1795, firstly to Lochmaben and then to the New Greyfriars Kirk in Edinburgh, crowning his career as Moderator of the General Assembly in 1813. Andrew Brown died in 1834 and is buried in Greyfriars Kirkyard. A cottage adjoining Sillerknowe was in the late eighteenth century home to a seer called Euphane Aitken, a contemporary of the above Richard Brown. She is said to have correctly predicted the location of the death of John Blake, itinerant killer, at Duncangill Head near Lamington. George Wilson had a workshop at Sillerknowe in 1876, Adam White, joiner and undertaker in the 1890s and in 1898 it was Pillan's yard. A burgh record of 1867 mentions Jenny Bell's Rig which ran behind Sillerknowe. The rig was to be used for storing Wilson's wood for which he had to pay £2.3/9d and 10/- storage or the wood would be sold.

The site was occupied by Aitken, slaters until around 1980. The reading and recreation club met upstairs in the 1940s in a room which had housed a few of the Polish Soldiers billeted in Biggar in 1940. The wall of No 154, the Chinese carry-out, has an unusual stone in its top right corner. It is a composite family celebration. The outer portion dates from 1773 for the marriage of Dr Willian Bow(e) to Rachel Deans and was probably rescued from their house which stood on or near that site. Bowe b.1723, Quothquan Mill, built the house in 1773 and married Rachel Deans of Chapelgill, Broughton in 1756. Dr Bowe was noted for giving his services to the poor of the district free of charge. Bowe died in 1790 but was followed in medicine by his son James who died in 1802. The inner portion of the stone is dedicated to the above George Wilson, his wife Elizabeth Aitchison and their seven children and dated 1886. George's name survives in George Square a short distance to the east.

The area to the east of Sillerknowe towards George Square was from 1792 the horse market. Stallions to be traded were segregated from the rest of the market transactions as stoned horses (horses with stones; uncastrated) caused havoc mixing with people and other beasts.

No 156 was the location of Andrew Black's blacksmith business since, at least, 1841. By 1851 he was employing three men including journeyman Thomas Binner. Business ex-

Nos 144-152, 1960s. On the right - Ferguson's grocery, on the left – Aitken's slater's yard.

vate house by 1925 when it became the home of Provost Donald Martin. The railing around the cellar entrance and stair were removed in 1954. William Haldane's garage sign was a prominent feature of the west gable of the building.

The space to the east of No 134 was filled in 1909 by Alexander Weir and sons and their plumbers' business at **Nos 136, 138 and 140**. The building is of brick but with a Dumfriesshire sandstone front. The design was by L.A. Morrison. Weirs remained in business until the 1980s. The great landscape painter, William Crozier (1897-1930) was a nephew of Alex Weir. To the rear of this block is Weir Court which was the site of a nineteenth century lodging house and the remaining buildings supported roll-moulding stones and a seventeenth century window before renovation.

No 142 is known as Cleuch Cottage, named by the Andersons of the Cleuch who stayed here c.1870. Thomas Harlan was here in 1880 before moving down to Floral Cottage. Prior to that it belonged to two George Stringers, father and son, who were house painters. The cottage once featured a fine early 19th century (or earlier) rosette on the vestibule ceiling. This was shaped like a star (in the manner of a garter star) with a medallion in the centre and with a seated female surrounded by other figures. Behind 142, up Sillerknowe Lane, was the house of William Haldane the coachbuilder and Mrs Haldane's laundry.

The site of **No 144** is now occupied by a modern block of flats but was previously the site of a shop. Ovens the grocer started here (an advert of 1913 states an establishment in 1806), having moved from Glasgow and serving his apprenticeship in Biggar before flitting up to No 153 in 1855. He started married life next door at No 146. The Ferguson family who were in it until the 1970s started with two brothers who were Scotch Cuddies (peddlers) in England and did well enough to establish a shop in Biggar on an upper floor of Ord's property at West End (now a public garden). Their sister was their housekeeper. She married George Cook, a van driver. He liked a dram. When the brothers came to No 144 the son William Ferguson went to Edinburgh and Mr and Mrs Cook took over. Once William had been trained in Edinburgh he returned and was given the shop by his uncles. Ferguson, as with other grocers, blended his own whisky. The Cooks stayed in No 146 and the brothers and another sister bought Wallacefield at no 184. William Ferguson lived in Howieson Square when first married. He had two sons and five daughters and was Baron Bailie for many years being active at the time of the public park and golf course inauguration in 1907. He resigned from the council in the 1920s and died in 1930. His son, also William continued the business until the 1970s.

Records of 1789 for **Nos 146 and 148** indicate a building being called Langstable at 146, owned by James Scott and occupied

The rear of Nos 130-134 – the White Hart. John Rae's 'herring field' garden.

The Auld Corse Knowe. Shenk's lithograph from an 1807 sketch by John Pairman published in 'Biggar and the House of Fleming'.

knowe was composed by John Pairman in 1807. The open space was used for travelling shows and the site is still used as the focus of the annual August shows and Hogmanay bonfire.

The cross-knowe was not the only knowe on the street. A short distance to the north-east were two smaller hillocks – the Tron Knowe where the public weighing beam was located and where all weighable ware e.g. butter, cheese, etc. was sold and the Siller Knowe where deals were done and money changed hands. The June fair, a cattle market, was known as the Skirling-Biggar fair, the Skirling Fair having had its last appearance in Skirling in 1861.

No 128 is the most visible representation of the old line of the High Street before nineteenth century encroachments were built. R&R Clark, William Pillans, and D and M Aitken and sons, slaters from June 1882 and another Aitken, a painter, are former occupants of this house. The line continues through Weir Court and in William Hunter's youth in the early 1800s he recalled the businesses of Robert Scott the saddler, William Steele, the blacksmith and the school run by former weaver John Slimon where Hunter received his primary education.

Nos 130, 132 and 134. The White Hart Inn was one of the first buildings to encroach on the High Street from its former line. The Baron Court minutes state – march between Admiral Fleming and John Steel who proposes building a new house in front of his old one 8th April 1837 – White Hart. The Bowling Club minutes of 1838 indicate their meetings were held there. John Porteous was the inn keeper in 1851. It was reported to be in very good repair in 1858 and by 1865 was run by Mungo Ferguson. The house adjacent, No 134, was added by John Steel in 1865 and is of a finer masonary finish. John Brown, the tailor was an early occupant of this house. He was the great-grandson of Jean Armour's sister. Steele, a veterinary surgeon, sold the White Hart in 1880 to William Russell and it became a temperance hotel run by George Ferguson with part of the building being run as a lodging house by Edward (Ned) McKinlay housing eighteen lodgers in 1881. Ned was born in County Tyrone in 1805 and could remember the victory over Napoleon at Waterloo. By 1904, at the age of 99, he became Biggar's oldest resident but died aged 101 in 1906. The garden behind the White Hart was known as the herring field. Herring, offal and other rubbish from the house fertilized the garden and produced great growth of potatoes planted by John Rae the bootmaker across the road although they were rumoured to be all shaws, no tubers! Rae kept his beehives here and his son, Michael had a lean-to greenhouse which was the forerunner of his market garden on South Back Road. The building later had a spell as Biggar Library and in 1918 became the food office where ration book applications were processed. It had become a pri-

Biggar High Street in 1861, just after the building of the new Corn Exchange

The Jubilee Fountain erected in 1887 and removed in 1947.

three years, from 1752 to 1836 the custom was held on December 18th as Biggar refused (for this purpose) to change from the Julian to Gregorian calendar; it had been held on December 31st for hundreds of years before that and has been ever since. The bonfire was reputed to have curative effects on humans and animals. Robert Pairman recalled around 1862 a foundered horse (with laminitus, a foot disorder) being ridden through a fringe of the fire to great public applause. In March 1880 a special bonfire was lit to celebrate WE Gladstone's victory in the General Election following his Midlothian Campaign. Children were noted to join the festivities by exploding turpentine balls!

Kitchen fires were at one time extinguished on Hogmanay to be re-lit by flames from the bonfire. A sketch of the cross

new bell and a wine cellar for the Biggar Club was built in 1898. In the 1890s the business of exchanging corn came to an end and it was sold to Robert Daybell around 1920 whose sister ran it as the Biggar Cinema. In 1935 it was gifted to the Burgh Council but it has continued as a venue for entertainment ever since. In the 1930s the cinema showed films on five occasions a week. Performers included Richard Tauber and Harry Lauder. It closed as a cinema in 1960.

Immediately in front of the Corn Exchange was the Jubilee Fountain built in 1887 to celebrate fifty years of Queen Victoria's reign. By as early as 1900 it had been described as a white elephant and there were calls for its removal. It was removed in 1947 but the four small boys astride water-spouting dolphins were rescued by Nessie Cuthbertson, wife of James A Cuthbertson and have since been preserved by Biggar Museum Trust. The boys were in fact modelled on a girl – Jean Lindsay, daughter of the station master. Her uncle, James Lindsay, a draughtsman with Steven and MacDowell, Ironfounders, designed and built the fountain.

To the north-east of the meal market was the Cross Knowe. It was around 7 to 10m in height and topped by the merkat cross. The cross had a masonry base 1.1m high with a plain shaft rising above it. The cross stone had a hole in the centre and date 1632. Its square apex had vertical sun-dials on four sides and initials J.E.W. – John Earl of Wigtoun and date 1694. State documents, acts of the Bailie's Court (local government) and notice of various fairs were posted at the cross. It was a meeting place for townsfolk and a play area for the youth of the day. As the central point of open markets which attracted people from the surrounding countryside on market days it was the centre of the town's activity. On snowy or frosty days children would slide down its slopes performing the hurley-hacket, a human-chain sledge (originally on a horse's skull) which often continued well down the street. Bonfires were lit to celebrate victories during the Napoleonic Wars and on one occasion over-enthusiastic youths extended the bonfire to the top of the cross pedestal, the heat from which cracked the shaft of the merkat cross and it had to be taken down. The cross stone and apex were rescued and in 1860 built into the south facing wall of the Corn Exchange. The pedestal and the knowe itself were removed in 1823 to make way for a new hotel which was never built but caused great regret among a number of local poets who lamented its loss e.g. Robert Rae's, 'A Yammerin' Auld Man's Lament for Biggar Auld Corse-knowe.' A depiction of the knowe on the Ordnance Survey map of 1858 suggests its remnants were still visible at that time. The contemporary Name Book describes a 'slight elevation'. A bonfire was also lit on top of the cross knowe each Hogmanay. Attempts were made as long ago as 1867 to have the custom discontinued as it was deemed dangerous to neighbouring buildings. For eighty-

No 118 was a butcher's business from 1864 till c.1980.

1893 and was succeeded by his son Andrew, daughter Cecilia and his youngest son, James who died in 1950. The business was taken over by George C Spiers and later his son-in-law. The continuing business has therefore been run by only two families in the past 160 years.

Nos 122, 124 and 126 was where Teenie Ling sold her homemade toffee balls in the 1880s and in 1894, after a tentative plan in 1890, William Hislop, watchmaker built in the angle of the two houses forming a room/dining room with an ornate plaster ceiling (and a bed recess in the 1890 plan). This became the famous Corner Shop occupied by Mrs Kate Peebles for 38 years. Hislop also built the kitchen at right angles to the back of the house. After Mrs Peebles retired the business was bought by Mr Ricci (Townhead Café) and in 1961 the corner room was gutted along with the house (No 122) and made into one shop. Norman Shannon, architect also had an office in No 122 before the amalgamation.

The **Corn Exchange** is the most conspicuous building on Biggar High Street. It was built in 1860 to a design by architect David McGibbon, by Jack and White of Edinburgh on the site of an old meal house. The meal house was a small one-storey, slated building standing immediately to the south-west of the Cross Knowe and opened each Thursday (market day constituted in 1451 in Biggar's Burgh of Barony charter) and on other occasions for sales of other commodities as and when required. However, by the mid-nineteenth century it had become infested with rats and mice. A dispute between Nicol Porteous, the toll keeper and William Brechan, a baker led the sheriff to impound a quantity of oatmeal in the meal house – a glorious arrangement for the rats and mice and the influence for James Affleck, the town poet, to write an 'Address of the Rats and Mice'. (See appendix).

The old meal house became almost useless and some leading burghers organised subscription shares for a new Corn Exchange. Shares of £5 each, snapped up by mainly farmers and merchants, were issued to pay for the new enterprise. The new build was on the site of the old meal house and adjoining land bought from Col John Fleming. The foundation stone was laid on 24th August, 1860 with full masonic honours following a grand procession, with instrumental band, from the mill, down the West Row and up the High St via the South UP (Gillespie) Church. The crow step-gabled Scots Jacobean front is faced with masonry of large whinstone blocks and sandstone rybats. The Corn Exchange was an immediate success providing the agricultural community with clean, light and airy accommodation for Thursday sales as well as committee rooms upstairs and from the beginning the spacious business hall was used by other organisations for dances, concerts and public entertainment. The gas illuminated clock was added in September 1882 along with a

Nos 108-110 – a chip shop since the 1930s but had many uses prior to that. The original premises of Robert Boa in 1858 and one of the first buildings to encroach on the southern side of the High Street.

style of architecture, two storeys high, slated and in very good repair'. David Thomson became the manager of the bank in 1857, having previously been the Western Bank agent.

Nos 108 and 110 (**Bank Place**) date from the 1820s and the eastern part was the original premises of Robert Boa before moving up to No 120 in 1864. Annand of Lanark's lawyer's office was in the western part in the 1870s. It housed a meal merchant, James Gibson in the 1880s Later, around 1900, the left hand side of the building was R Murray the tailor's and Charles Stewart's cycle shop to around 1925; right - H Lothian, fishmonger and greengrocer, then Mrs Murray's grocers' in 1946. Mrs SW Frame ran the business till 1951 when Margaret Linton took over. It has also been a motor garage at one time. A Tait occupied the property at the same time as Lothian. This may be the partner of William Haldane, coachbuilders of North Back Road and whose advertising sign occupied the western gable of the White Hart Inn. The first fish and chip shop arrived with Dick Cole in the 1930s closely followed by Barbara and Richard Combe.

No 114 was occupied by William Hislop the watchmaker in 1880 to be succeeded by his son, also William who was to become Provost of Biggar in the 1920s, AM Lawson the florist in the 1950s and became Jimmy Ritchie's electrical shop in the 1970s.

The block from **Nos 116 to 120** was built c.1864 and occupied by Joseph Bertram, grain merchant who moved from 119 across the street. It was taken over by Walter Brunton, butcher in 1866 (see 17 High St). David Dickson succeeded Brunton on his retiral in 1884. He was father of John L Dickson, Corstane, Broughton who began the export killing at Biggar and later built his own slaughterhouse at Broughton. The slaughter business kept the railway line open after passenger traffic had ceased. Dickson was succeeded by 1911 by John Graham, by the 1920s by Mr Younger and by the 1950s by Linton Bros, sons of Wm Linton, grocer at No 133 and ceasing to be a butcher's shop by around 1980. The garden to the rear of Nos 116-118 is occupied by an eighteenth century columbarium or doocot which would have added pigeon meat to the regular diet of the population.

No 120 was occupied by Robert Boa, born in Lanark in 1837, who moved up in 1864 from 108 where he had been since 1853. There is a cellar beneath. In 1869 the Burgh Commissioners ordered the steps to be removed from the block as an encroachment on the street. The property was then owned by David Lockhart (No 131). The plan showed two 4½" steps at Brunton's. Lockhart proposed one step 7 or 8". The street slope was also altered at Hislop's and the Royal Bank. The signage above the shop door is the 1864 original made at McFarlane's Saracen Iron Works in Glasgow. Robert died in

ner with Gladstone and Core, as a ladies outfitter till 1937 when she flitted to Victoria Buildings. Michael Rae then moved up from No 88 and was there till his death. The house upstairs was used by Smail and Ewart when they moved up from No 50. Mr Ewart's room, where weddings were performed, was the left hand one upstairs (up-street) above the hairdresser's shop. William Ewart joined the solicitors' firm in 1912. He was born in 1882 and his intrepid parents took him on a voyage from Liverpool to Portland, Oregon in *The Annesley*, a three-masted sailing ship, around Cape Horn! The Panama Canal had not been completed at that time. Smail and Ewart flitted in 1958/9 to the old Commercial Hotel and upstairs and downstairs were re-converted to houses. The downstairs shop, after Michael Rae's death was used by Smail and Ewart as Burgh Rates Office, being occupied by John Russell, Burgh Chamberlain and the windows were used by RE Watson, the hairdresser and proprietor next door. The hairdresser's shop No 96 was in the 1850s Matthew Ramsay's Apothecaries' Hall succeeded by Alexander Tennant, John Lindsay and Aaron Whitfield in 1865. It was occupied in 1880 by Walter Rae and James Adams (1839-1901) who was established in the 1860s. Adams went there with his barber's pole and fish (for fishing tackle) (originally in Gibson's Close with a bleeding bowl man). After that Donald Adams the son, who had a short leg and an iron extension on his boot, sold musical instruments such as melodeons and fiddles besides being a barber and tobacconist. He died in the 1938 and was succeeded by Robert E Watson his assistant who had also a ladies salon in the same premises.

No 98 was another building with a good stucco mantelpiece with sheep, garlands and an eagle at either end manufactured in the fashion described above but was marred with brown paint. Miss Don was tenant having moved after her father's death from No 84 and had a good collection of her mother's watercolours.

No 100 was once a 'gentleman's draper' belonging to Peter Brown and R Murray from the 1850s. Then McMath, the grocer had it from 1889 to around 1910. When Lindsay Bros took over, shifting up from No 92, the front shop was refreshed in the art nouveau style, panelled in unvarnished mahogany-stained wood to about 1½ ft from the ceiling with a small ledge all around the top. The panels were grey stipple, alternating with a heavy gold and pink conventional lily flower. The ledge continued around the partition to the back shop which had at one time a bead curtain.

The Western Bank first owned **No 104** after moving over the road from No 105. When the Western collapsed in 1857 the Royal Bank took over. This was another villa-like building using ashlar sandstone, described in the Ordnance Survey Name Book as 'a very commodious building in the modern

Nos 92-94 – Peter Reivley and an apprentice at Lindsay Bros c.1900.

Nos 78-100 (pre-Post Office). Rt to l – Wilson, stationer; Linn, grocer; McMath, grocer; Dickson, draper; Rae, bootmaker; Lindsay, painter; Adams, barber, Brown and Murray, drapers.

shop between Graham and Wilson the bakers (site of 101 High St). He was there in 1879, then crossed to No 96 and was later at No 88 where his son Michael carried on till he had to move to No 92 around1937. At all these places he had a Servant's Registry (recruitment agencies for domestic servants) and on fair days there was always a crowd round his door. This humane practice eventually killed off the old hiring methods.

Attractive pillars mark the entrance to **Nos 92 and 94**. An old fashioned shop signboard above the pillars is still in position but not in use. The room downstairs at No 92 had until 1959 a pine and stucco mantelpiece fashioned in the usual Biggar manner which is not as effective as the better known 'Adam style' type. In this case there were two mantels both ornamented, one above the other. The ornaments were eagles (1815?) and flowers and were much broken and not really worth preserving. Being in the shop part of the building they had been subject to much abuse and brown paint. The room immediately upstairs had a Victorian wood mantel and a delicate oval plaster garland around the ceiling. This was Smail and Ewart's office and waiting room. In 1864 Wm Hislop, watchmaker moved from here to No 114. When Hislop left in 1864 another watchmaker, Matthew Robertson came across from No 87. Watchmakers seem to have followed one another around a great deal. He was a son of Matthew Robertson (1796-1855), grocer at Townhead, a relative of the Johnstones, bakers and the Blakes who went to Greenock and were grandparents of George Blake the author (The Shipbuilders). Robertson went to Glasgow in the 1870s and had a business in St Vincent St. He died at Shettleston in 1910 aged 75. His widow was Christina Pairman.

After Robertson, came Lindsay Bros., house painters. Walter and his twin John George were sons of the coachman at Biggar Park. They split up in 1877 when John went to Galashiels where he rose to being a bailie. Walter remained in Biggar and was its most popular and enterprising provost. He became provost and Justice of the Peace in 1894 and a lieutenant in the Lanarkshire Rifle Volunteers, one of their best shots. He married twice and by his first wife (a Brunton) had two sons John N and Walter B who were also 'Lindsay Bros'. John was responsible for the stencilling on the shop front c.1903. The bottom band and chequer pattern were in purple and the lettering in black. Lindsay Bros' glass sign is behind the present unused shop sign. In about 1918 the business removed to No 100. Walter senior stayed in the house above No 92 till he bought Kerfield on Mid Road in 1891. John and his wife Peg, daughter of Archie Sommerville, carter stayed in the old house until after Walter senior's widow died. Kerfield was sold after his death in the 1940s.

The shop was then occupied by Miss Roberts, a former milli-

Nos 86, 88, and 90. In 1876 JL Murray's plans were passed by the Burgh Commissioners for James Brunton to build a grocers shop, a new building between Peter Brown's and the property of Mrs Pairman. The site had hosted Dr Pairman's first surgery before moving to No 72. The shop at the Neilson Bridge falling vacant at the time however, the Bruntons established their business there though they retained this building and let it. Mr JD Brown bought it from the Brunton family in the early 1950s. The building consists of two shops and two houses (later made into one) above. The one next to the Post Office buildings was for many years from the 1880s used by Robert M Dickson the draper. The dressmakers worked upstairs and Mrs Adams, working there in 1896 witnessed TB Murray's first motor car drive up Biggar High Street. Dickson was partnered with Peter Brown (No 100) before setting up on his own here. His wife was a daughter of Baron Bailie Robertson's son James Robertson, a builder. She had the siller and was fond of reminding Robert - "Remember where the money comes from". She had her grand–father's property at Townhead and some riggs (cultivation plots) along the Mid Road which she sold to RG Murray at a small price as he would just have taken them if she hadn't accepted his offer. (Legal titles could be very difficult to establish in those days so this happened many times; a lot of the owners could no longer identify their property). RM Dickson was on the school board and a great supporter of Rev John Scott whose speeches were written by Mrs Dickson. Their three sons were all well-travelled. George in South Africa married a widow with a family and had one daughter who had several relics of the baron bailie. Robert was the art master at Harris Academy and James Robertson died in 1967. A Mr Arthur came to sell off the stock in the 1920s. He specialised in this work having previously done the same at No143. He kept the business running under his own name and his daughter (d.1970) married John D Brown, elder son of James Brown, tailor, 134 High St., a former apprentice ironmonger with Gilbert Rae. He set up as 'Hatter, hosier, draper, outfitter, auctioneer and valuator'. In 1937 he took over Walter Rae's shop next door as the gent's department and enlarged his own house upstairs in about 1950. His only daughter, Jean was Fleming Queen in 1938, married Walter Pollock and emigrated to Malaya. The Pollocks returned in 1960/1 and, after a short partnership, succeeded JD Brown in 1962 as sole proprietors. The smaller shop was let to Walter Rae who took over Mr Hogg's bootmaker's business and was occupied by him and his son from about 1885-1936. The houses upstairs, merged in 1950 or thereabouts, were occupied prior to that by Gavin Cree, nurseryman and family (above 88) and John D Brown. Walter and John Rae were bootmakers from Carmichael educated by Thomas Braidwood who was famous in his day for his teaching excellence. Walter started business in a small

JL Murray's front elevation drawing of the Post Office built 1898.

shire sandstone. Burgh Commissioners records – " John Brown Jnr, Boghall, permission to remove public well (Malcolm's Well) in front of buildings to be erected and he will dig a well where the commissioners want – this was to be opposite between the easternmost tree on the north side of the street and the lamp post. The new pavement to be 6-8" lower than at present." The buildings at the back were built in 1876. Malcolm's well sat at the front of an open space known as Greenland Square (possibly because of the grass growing on the thatched roofs of the adjacent cottages). James Toward, son of Walter of the Crown, ran the Clydesdale Hotel with his two sisters from the 1880s till 1901 and Max Wells and David Maxwell, Agnes Duncan, Gavin Wilson, Duncan Mclean in the early twentieth century. The General's Bar to the rear was named after General MacArthur, a play on the name of Alec MacArthur the owner in the 1980s.

Miss Angelina Brown and her brother George had a bazaar next door at No78 until 1890 when John H Wilson the bookseller, son of John Wilson the baker, started a long sequence of shops of that ilk. Wilson had been David Lockhart's assistant and on his death in 1899 the business was run by his widow the redoubtable Mrs Margaret Wilson with Mr Kent her printer. Mrs Wilson stayed in the Post Office building above and had a speaking tube installed to communicate with her maid. Mrs Wilson was succeeded by Jimmy Telfer and from around 1969, Ian Hamilton.

Nos80, 82, 84 - the Post Office Buildings. The 1898, JL Murray two-storey building plus attics (built for the Biggar Auction Market Company) has finely executed dormer heads but recent neglect of the gutters has left the building water-stained and in need of some tender loving care. The foundation stone was laid on 22nd July 1898 by James C Hozier MP and its first postmaster was John Logan followed by A Provan in 1913. A new sorting room enlarged the building in 1905 and the telephone exchange in the 1930s. An earlier telephone exchange was located inside the Post Office door. The exchange worked till 1973 and is now in Biggar Museum. Before 1898 Robert Linn, provision merchant was at No80 and another grocer, Miss Jeannie McMath at No84. After 1898 it continued as a grocer's shop in a new guise under the occupancies of John Hislop, Albert Horsburgh till 1967, John Wilson till 1992 and E Kelly. Between Nos 82 and 84 is Tinny Calder's Close. This was the home and workshop from the 1830s of William Calder (born in Dunbar in 1797) the tinsmith who, with his great friend, Wattie Gray, posed for an iconic photograph by Menzies Moffat. One of the first families to occupy the flats above the 1898 building was that of Alexander B Don, a maths and science teacher at Biggar High School. His wife, Tessie, who had six children including Dora Don the primary school teacher, was a talented water-colour artist.

Some images around the foot of Kirkstyle.

Left - c.1880 showing the newly completed Clydesdale hotel.

Below left – a George Allan image from the 1950s with the Lido café in the Cafolla's day.

Below right – carriages parked outside the Clydesdale hotel on Show Day August 1888.

combination of a chemist's shop, a veterinary outlet, perfumery and delicatessen selling products as varied as Burt's heartburn tablets, Parr's life pills, laudanum, physic balls for horses, arsenic, Eau de Cologne, Prince Albert's pomade, cinnamon and Cayenne pepper. Dr Pairman died in 1873. The building became Toward's Hotel in 1901, run by Walter Toward's daughters, having moved from the Clydesdale Hotel with their brother James, a sign for which is still visible beside the present hotel sign. The building became Dr William Lindsay's, who fell victim to the 'flu' epidemic of 1919, then Drs Robert and William Marshall's home and surgery in the mid-twentieth century and later an Abbeyfield Home. The brick washhouses behind No 70 are still intact.

The Church of Scotland's **Gillespie Centre** was built as the South United Presbyterian Church in 1877 by Hope and Kerr to a design by John Lamb Murray (1838 – 1908). Murray was from a farming family at Heavyside and was Biggar's premier nineteenth century architect. His practice moved to Edinburgh and he went on to design an extension to Hamilton County Buildings in the 1870s and the Shotts Lunatic Asylum in 1890. He also built the Heavyside Wheel to drain the Biggar gap with James Watt and a water-powered organ in his Heavyside home. A stained glass window was dedicated to him in Biggar Kirk in 1910.

The Gillespie Church, named after the Rev Thomas Gillespie an eighteenth century dissenter and founder of the Scottish relief church, opened 1878 and cost £4,200. The Burgh Commissioners recorded – *"A dyke to be built from Clydesdale Hotel to Mrs Pairman's (Morven) and a private footway. Ground to be valued for compensation. A public path to be allowed if privileges not abused"*. The original SUP church, built in 1781 by seceeders or dissenters from the parish church, by private subscription of the congregation, sat back from the present Gillespie Centre and to the west, partially behind the Kirkstyle Hotel on the original line of the High St. The congregation met in the Corn Exchange during the re-building phase. The wraggle on the wall of the Clydesdale Hotel to the east marks the position of a former house owned by the Kennedy family which was demolished to make way for the new church and the Kennedys rehoused with compensation. The new Kennedy house, Church Cottage, sits immediately behind the Gillespie centre and the variety of random stone rubble used in the gable end construction suggests that some stone from the old house was used in its construction. At the front of the church carved stone heads of Martin Luther and John Knox straddle the ogee-arched and crocketed hood-mould front entrance. The Gillespie was the preferred place of worship for the ordinary working folk of Biggar.

Nos 74, 76, 78 the Clydesdale Buildings from a JL Murray design of 1875 for the Biggar Auction Company and Walter Toward was the first major building in Biggar to use Dumfries-

Forte's Cyclist's Rest, also known as the Lido Café at No 64. 1920s.

James Tweedie the draper at No 60 on the site of the 1932 Co-op building.

of bank agent as well as being a lawyer, in 1846. He was commissioned Baron Bailie of the Burgh of Biggar and elected 1st magistrate of the Police Burgh of Biggar in 1863. Paul also served as clerk to the Biggar and Leadhills Turnpike Trust and treasurer of the Biggar Savings Bank, Athenaeum, Gas Coy., Horticultural Soc., Biggar and Symington Railway Coy., amongst other local organisations – a real pillar of the community. Paul's brother John of Cambuswallace was to follow as manager on Thomas's death followed by Messrs Kello, Smith, Cairns and Draper. The gates were added around 1930 by Aitchison the blacksmith.

The Lanark Co-operative Society Store was built at **Nos 60-62** in 1931/2, with garages and later extension, by William Mercer, SCWS architect Glasgow. Before that, a row of single storey buildings stood there and included No 60, the business of James Tweedie the draper in the 1880s and around 1900, Mary Gair the fruiterer followed by Poletti's toy shop. The co-op's corporate design at the time included the use of marble and sparkling larvikite granite. Plastic signage detracted from this fine finish but the 1930s stonework is still visible. In the early days of the Co-op it held its own annual day out for its members and they and their children would follow the band hired especially for the occasion marching to the public park where great fun and games were had.

Now a private house, **No 64** was the home of John Lindsay, the chemist in the 1880s followed by James Tweedie, the draper in September 1892. Alfonso & Celestine Forte's Cyclist's Rest, famed for its ice cream and confectionary, took it into the twentieth century. It was known as the Lido Café from around 1927 and Forte's nephew Andrew Cafolla continued the business. A fleet of tricycles with freezer boxes delivered ice cream to the near district. Next door at **No 66** was Kennedy the saddler, selling to Andrew Selkirk and later becoming Miss Brunton's haberdashery. Madelaine Brunton opened the Chocolate Bowl after retiral from Biggar High School.

No72, the Kirkstyle Hotel has shuttled back and forth between the medical and hostelry professions. Built around 1850 with 1880s extensions when the old South UP Church was demolished, it was, as Morven, Dr Robert Pairman's laboratory. Pairman born in Biggar 1818, son of Robert Pairman, merchant in Biggar, was one of the town's most prominent residents. He left medical school in Edinburgh with distinguished honours and immediately settled back in Biggar to practise. He put his mind to researching and writing an 'Exposition of Asiatic Cholera' but sadly attributed it to a damp and foul atmosphere rather than the infected water supplies which were later discovered to be the cause. He had more success with 'Fever Poisons in our Streets and Homes' which became a major teaching resource. His dispensary was in the room to the left but it was more than that. It was a

Forrest the baker at Nos 26-28 in the 1930s. Wilson's tea room at no 29 is on the right.

butchers. Aaron died in 1873 and his widow carried on till Oct 1878 when she disposed of the business to RG Stewart. Later it passed to Thomas McFarlane who amongst other accomplishments manufactured aerated water. He was followed by John Eunson from Orkney who flitted to No48 when the shop still continued as a chemist's in charge of Robert McAllister from May 1892 then John S Dempster who came from Peebles. On Dempster's death he disposed of his business to an assistant of Eunson's, John L Budge who tragically died by his own hand in the store at the rear of the shop on New Year's day 1952. Since then the owners have been Mr and Mrs Fraser McDonald and Tom Matthews. Mr McDonald used No50 as an ophthalmic saloon. It had formerly been Jean Dempster's hairdressing shop and stood empty for some years.

No56 was built as a branch of the Commercial Bank of Scotland by David Rhind in 1836. It is a two storey villa in the late Georgian style employing ashlar sandstone with a single storey 20th century extension. Thomas Paul occupied the post

No 44- Thomas Shiels sign revealed during renovations in the 1990s.

No38 has a large curved plate glass window facing down the lower part of the street, making full use of the awkward site. The entrance to these buildings has a fine mosaic pavement. It was occupied by Dickson the confectioner in the 1910s and '20s then Abe Mitchell's second-hand emporium and the home bakery of Miss Stephen. No 42 was the labour exchange in 1936 bearing a rare and ephemeral Edward VIII government plaque and then became the Co-op's drapery department.

Nos 44, 46 and 48 date from the 1880s with rear additions in 1896. In the 1880s No44 was the business of Thomas Watson the shoemaker followed by Gilbert Chalmers and Thomas Shiels (1859-1924). Shiels was one of some twenty boot and shoemakers in Biggar in 1896 and known as 'Terrible Tom' on account of his notorious temper. John Ramsay, cabinet-maker was there from 1960. No 48 was Tweedie the draper's shop. James Tweedie was of a family of joiners and apprenticed to Adam Pairman (No 81) at the same time as William Gladstone, who was his best man, in the early 1870s. His daughter married William Johnston. John Eunson the chemist flitted here in February 1892 from No 54 and stayed above the shop. His son, also a chemist, died there unmarried. He was a former member of the dramatic club and keen organiser of the poppy day collection for the British Legion. He had a photographic dark room which could be used for developing and printing by amateurs.

Nos 50 and 52 housed Andrew Smail's (of Smail and Ewart) office for many years. No52 was his house, built 1885 by James Tweedie with later addition and No 54 his original lodgings. When Miss Whitfield disposed of her business she had had a lodger for nearly two years in the person of Andrew Smail, a native of Eddleston who had served a legal apprenticeship with Blackwood and Smith of Peebles and who had started work in Barrhill. He came to Biggar in 1877. There was then no proper lawyer in the place and he did good business. On the death of David Lockhart (No131) he became registrar and remained in that post until his death in 1927. His main claim to local celebrity is his similarly long period as Town Clerk. During his term of office most of the town improvements were carried out. He joined the congregation of Moat Park church until the organ was introduced in 1910 when he left and went to the Gillespie, who unfortunately followed their sister congregation's lead shortly later, much to his annoyance. Smail's office later became Biggar's first ladies' hairdresser.

No 54 was a Whitfield property. Alan Whitfield in the Kirkstyle was the postmaster. Aaron Whitfield, son of Alan, was a druggist here in 1865. He built 'New Apothecaries Hall' property in March 1871. The new building was to be 25' from the centre of the street. Whitfield's business papers tell us that his supply of lard for ointments came from local

ELEVATION

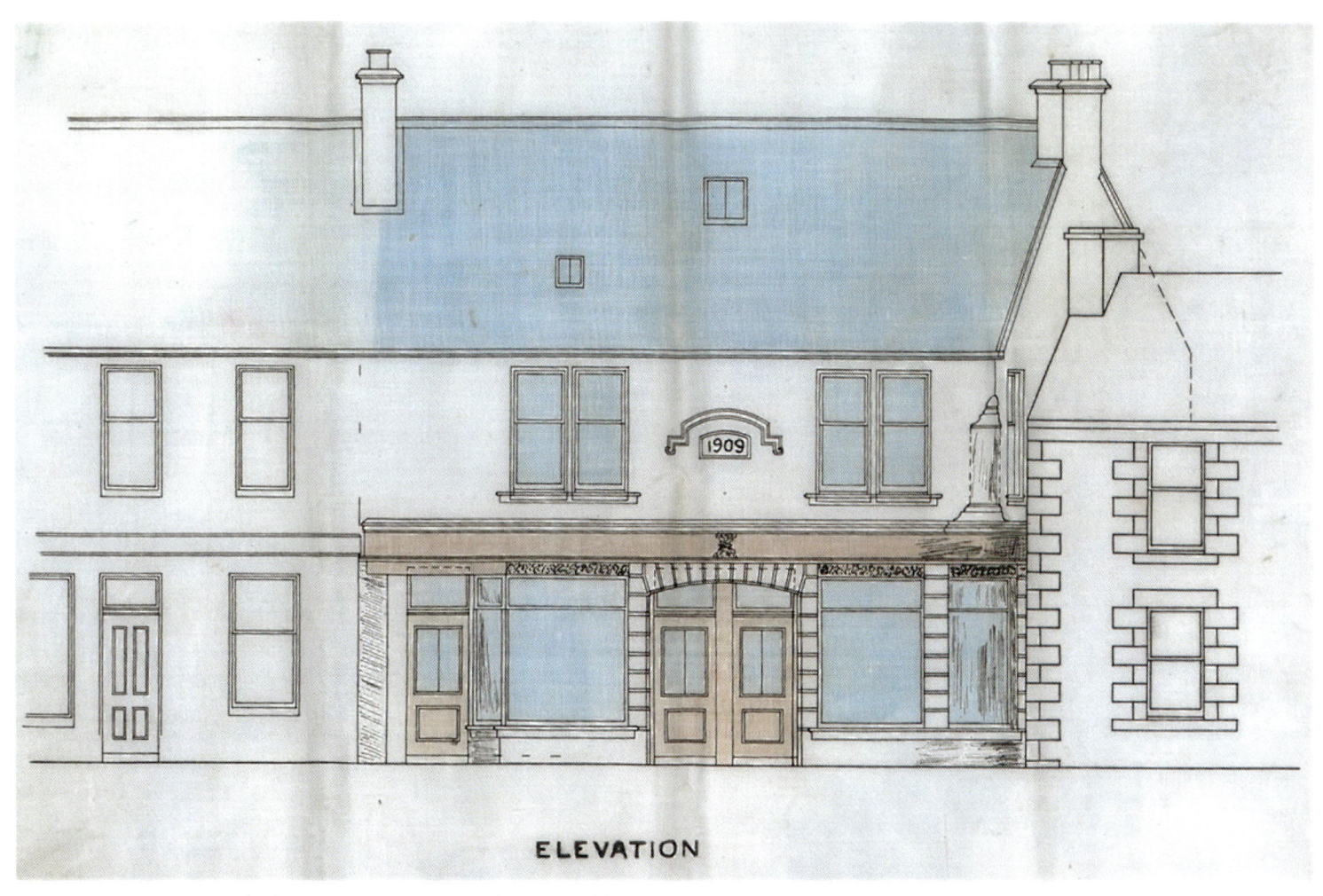

Nos 38-42 LA Morrison's design on a site previously occupied by Brown and Jamieson's photographic studios.

mouldings rather like the old Elphinstone Hotel door but the owner inserted a glass panel in the top half. This door was in turn replaced by a hardwood door in 1978. A stone marked MV 1697 was found in the garden and is now built in to the bridge to Greenhill in the Burn Braes.

John Gladstone moved to around **Nos 34-36** between 1841 and 1851. He lived further up the street prior to this, round about the Post Office site (removed 1898). Brian Lambie noted the following: *The building consists of a shop and house and was I think the home of John Gladstone, watchmaker (d.1851) the cousin of (Prime Minister) Gladstone's father. If he was there in 1820 then the house can boast of sheltering the future prime minister under its roof as William Ewart Gladstone, on a visit with his father, Sir John stayed with the watchmaker and his family. In 1851 his widowed daughter-in-law and unmarried son, James, stayed with him and William Hislop had taken over the shop and stayed in that part of the building.* Hislop, who also sold barometers with his name plate attached, one of which was brought back to Biggar in 2003 from a dealer in Wales, later went to No94 and still later to No116.

In the 1890s the Allans had a flower shop there. The Misses Lambie of Hillridge took over a ladies' dressmaker's shop and in 1896 sold it to the Misses Logan of Knowhead whose business thrived until retiring to Ennerdale on Coulter Rd in about 1946. The Logans were agents for Pullars of Perth, the dry cleaners. Mrs Hunter and her sister Miss Colthart operated a gift shop for a few years when the standards in jewellery just after the war were very low. The business was profitable but gave up shop and house when their brother at Burghmuir died and they went to live there with Mrs Hunter's son Willie. After that Mrs Barbara Wilson, widow of Tom Wilson, baker conducted a dressmaking establishment with a high standard dress shop assisted by Miss Roberts' old assistant, Jean Graham. She retired in the late 1960s.

Nos 38-42 - a stone fronted brick building comprising two shops with flats above with an eye-catching date panel of 1909 designed by LA Morrison. Latto Alexander Morrison, b.1873, son of schoolmaster James Morrison, was John Lamb Murray's architectural assistant from 1886, became his partner in 1898 and married his daughter, Marion. When Murray retired in 1905 Morrison became sole partner. He has a fine stained-glass window dedicated to him on the west wall of Biggar Kirk. The building was erected on a vacant site except for a green shed with a red tin roof, the studio of Brown of Lanark from 1890 and later his assistant Jamieson, photographers. The hut was carted down to Station Road in 1909.

ding in 1947 the elder of the other two daughters, Bella, was present at the ceremony and took Rae's chrysanthemums to decorate the house for the countess's visitors (who included the King of Norway) and delighted them with her home baking. (Jeannie, Lady Antrim's maid, was a Mrs Haggard; her husband was cousin of the novelist, Rider Haggard.) She and Ailie, the other daughter, ran the business after their father's death in their own haphazard way. They had a motor van for a while which Ailie drove. They later bought-in Gibson's bread and only baked teabread and fancy baking. Ailie and Bella both died in 1978. Nobody could cater as well as they did for a social or dance but they worked all hours and were always at the last minute but never actually late. Their 'uniform' on such occasions was a white overall, white beret (as opposed to the dark, lop-sided berets they wore in the shop) or hat and white plimsolls or gutties. As an example of their endless toil Brian Lambie recalled the following: *'One Wednesday, Ailie went up to the bedroom and saw her Sunday coat lying on the bed. Only then did she realise that she hadn't been to bed since she had taken off her coat after the kirk on Sunday'*. As far as income tax went, the authorities gave them up as a bad job and many a local organisation was unable to balance its books because the Forrests hadn't cashed a cheque. They made the best wedding cakes in Biggar and though the decoration was a labour of love it was usually being done the night before. Their mother, once confronted by an irate lady brandishing a cut loaf with a fly in it, said "Fly? That's a current" and picked it out and ate it to prove it. Quick witted or apocryphal, the same tale was told of Mrs Wilson and of Peter the Great's baker!

No30 is one of the more distinctive houses on the street. It was divided up in the early twentieth century into one-up, one-down. The cast iron pillars at the front came from the old school on Kirkstyle c.1830s. Many a pupil was chastised against them (whipping post). Some of the Mitchells stayed here, and later the Abbots. The property till about 1945 was Miss Rae's who left it to her nephew Isaac Alcock. Jimmy Horne stayed upstairs till about 1949 and John Coupland (No119) till 1959. Upstairs was later sold to Mrs McMorran and downstairs to Mrs John Mitchell of the Post Office buildings.

Another very distinctive house whose ground floor exhibits probably the best masonry work in whinstone, sits next door at **No32**. Glenstraan, formerly Floral Cottage. Once the home of Thomas Harlan, the painter (1901-11), it was formerly a single storey cottage and William Minto said his grandfather the mason built it – this would have been around 1835. The original single storey gable end can be made out on the eastern side of the building and the upper storey stone work is of slightly poorer quality than the lower. The gothic pillars were matched by a door with pointed

Nos 22-24. The 2½-storey block next door had a house and shop downstairs and two houses upstairs. It was built for the Aitchisons in the late 1870s on the site of a small two-storey house and some open space or a garden which had a wooden fence round it. Part of the Tweedie garden site is now No26. The old house, with a door and window downstairs and only one window upstairs, was a cadjer's or carrier's place belonging to the Robb family of Parkgatestone who were connected to Mitchell the saddlers and jewellers, Lamb of the Cross Keys, and Minto, the coal agent.

In the new block was the house (the smaller of the two houses, No22, right-hand door), after his retiral, of James Crichton, headmaster of the old South School and his housekeeper Leezbeth Bertram, till he died in 1887. The shop downstairs was Maggie Sinclair's china establishment for about 40 years. Maggie took over from the Misses J&R Aitchison (china merchants) in 1900. Their doorbell plate survived upstairs until 1976. She looked after her uncle, David Gladstone of Rose Villa till his death in 1899. It was arguably the best china shop in Biggar selling fine Wemyss and Crown Derby ware. The shop was empty for a short time when James Johnstone, shoemaker took over. He flitted to Alex Clark's shop (No155) when Clark retired and No24 was taken by George Wilson, painter whose wife resumed the china shop business (later at No51). In their window was part of the Vitreolite sign of James Wilson and Sons, bakers removed from premises across the road when Bells took over (No27). Wilson later crossed to No 55 and Johnstone came back (he still stayed in the house next door) until his retiral in 1959. He would, in 1970, don his cobbler's apron again to star in a STV documentary about Gladstone Court Museum. Miss Alice Stewart, a member of the Campbell family of Nos 3-19, opened as a greengrocer and florist after Johnstone. She was succeeded c.1965 by John Elliot, former coal merchant and in the 1970s by Lynn Thorpe, but the Thorpes let it from about 1984 to Tina's Mini-market. By 1995 it was used as a funeral undertaker's.

Nos26-28 - Jubilee House. As its name suggests, this house was built in 1887 (Queen Victoria's golden jubilee) on the site of a 1½-storey house adjoining No30 and part of the garden already mentioned at No24. The shop and bakehouse built in 1887 were first occupied by John Dobbie. He came to Biggar around 1884 to succeed John Wilson, baker at No 27 and flitted to the new premises. His family did not continue in the business and William Forrest, the van man, took over. He had a horse van which was garaged up the adjacent pend and concluded every transaction by the remark "Weel I'll be poppin' on" earning him the nick-name 'auld pop-on'. One daughter was housekeeper to the Countess of Antrim, one of Queen Alexandra's ladies and at the present Queen's wed-

Tweedie the fruiterer at No 14.

WP Bryden, a grandson of Pillans the chief magistrate, bought it over around 1928, survived a fire of about 1936 and moved out around 1958 to Patrick's shop at 14 High St. He had other shops further up the street and cycled daily between them, 'no hands' all the way! Bryden became provost in the 1950s, hosted the Queen on her visit to Biggar in 1956 and lit the bonfire in 1974. He died in 1979. Nancy Farquhar moved into the shop from Station Road where she had managed a branch of the Bridge of Cally wool shops but ran her own High Street business.

No 8, Candy Cottage faces the Biggar Burn. It was built for James Brown of Candybank in 1857-8 from a design by millwright and architect James Watt. Brown was born at Rowhead in 1793, farmed at Candybank till 1864 and had become Biggar's oldest man when he died in 1888. The house is similar to Mayfield (beside Burghmuir on the Edinburgh side of the showfield) built for his brother Alex, around the same time. Candy Cottage has typical Watt features – a deep projecting of the edging stones on the corners and window frames. A plan survives in the Biggar and Upper Clydesdale Museum signed JW. Candybank, Rowhead Farm, Cormiston, the old South School and several more houses in the High St including the Masonic House are Watt's work. Brown was a bit of an antiquarian. His collection included a James V spur, a George I cavalry sword and several Neolithic stone tools from the surrounding area. Brown's son William, the coal merchant also lived there in 1881.

The Hamiltons of Poniel inherited the cottage and it was occupied for some time by John Paterson the market auctioneer (son William killed in 1917 at Ypres) and a famous Paul Roumeau clock (Smith's Scottish Clocks and Clockmakers) had its home here for many years. AC McNair, teacher of Latin and Scripture at Biggar High School, later provost and still later headmaster, lived here most of his married life. The Hamiltons sold it to John Hogg of Symington in 1947, who modernised the interior and ran a courier's business from the house. It was sold in 1968 or thereabouts to James P Weir, formerly a teacher at BHS and a retired headmaster. His widow built a porch on the front.

Mrs Tait, a grocer, traded from **No10** in the 1860s. **No14** had G Kelly trading in the nineteenth century. T Tweedie, the fruiterer was there in 1924 followed by Patrick and Bryden. Tweedie had a nursery on Station Road which supplied his tomatoes etc. **Nos16 and 18** respectively housed James Blair and Harland Bros with their clothier and tailoring businesses in 1880. Blair had been around since 1855.

The single storey house, **No20**, was occupied in 1960 by Miss Williamina Ramsay. It appears in an 1874 lithograph and a photograph taken around 1865.

Nos 2 and 4 in the 1880s – Brunton, grocer and Mitchell, saddler.

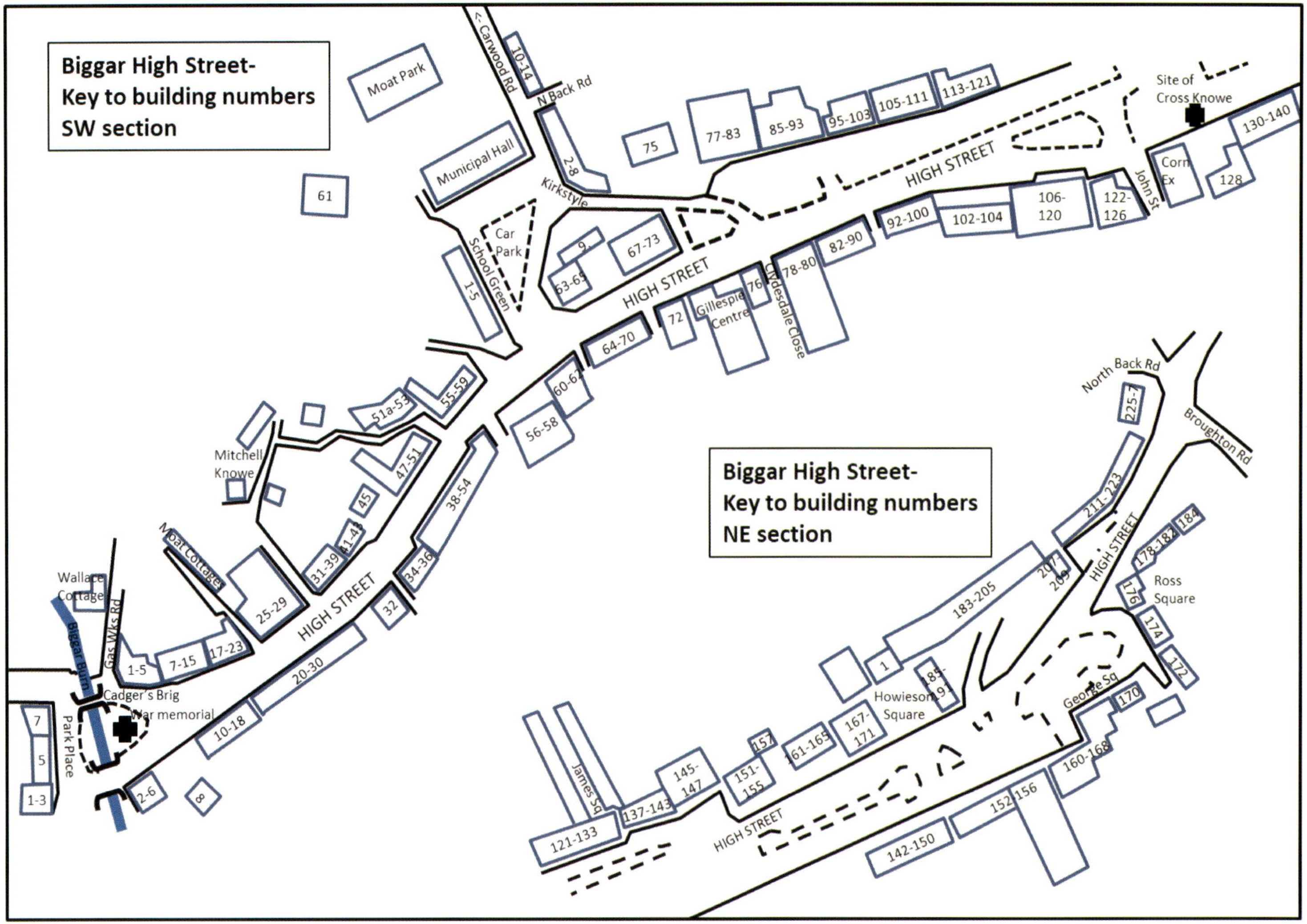
Biggar High Street-
Key to building numbers
SW section
Biggar High Street-
Key to building numbers
NE section
Moat Park
<- Carwood Rd
10-14
N Back Rd
Municipal Hall
2-8
Kirkstyle
61
Car
Park
School Green
1-5
9
63-65
67-73
HIGH STREET
75
77-83
85-93
95-103
105-111
113-121
HIGH STREET
Site of
Cross Knowe
130-140
Corn
Ex
128
John St
122-
126
106-
120
102-104
92-100
82-90
78-80
Clydesdale Close
76
Gillespie
Centre
72
64-70
60-62
56-58
55-59
51a-53
47-51
45
41-43
31-39
Mitchell
Knowe
Moat Cottage
25-29
HIGH STREET
38-54
34-36
32
20-30
10-18
2-6
8
Wallace
Cottage
Gas Wks Rd
Biggar Burn
1-5
7-15
17-23
Cadger's Brig
War memorial
7
5
1-3
Park Place
North Back Rd
Broughton Rd
225-7
211-223
HIGH STREET
184
178-182
176
Ross
Square
174
172
207-
209
183-205
1
185-
191
Howieson
Square
George Sq
170
160-168
167-
171
161-165
157
151-
155
145-
147
137-143
James Sq
121-133
HIGH STREET
142-150
152
156

lighting and drainage. Hitherto some lighting had been attempted but was pretty haphazard due to lack of funds and authority. In 1850 there were still only six gas lamps, all in private hands and therefore irregularly lit. Lanark and Peebles had a much better system and this prompted the campaign to have the system improved. The town would have to wait till 1883 for the first electric lighting to appear.

Before the coming of the Caledonian Railway in 1848 a common site on the High St was rows of lead ingots. They were carted from mines at Leadhills and Wanlockhead to Biggar where the mining companies had agents. Carters form Edinburgh and Leith would pick up the loads from Biggar and when supply was high Biggar carters would pick up some excess trade. In the region of 900 cart loads would have passed through Biggar each year.

To complement its first edition maps of Scotland, the Ordnance Survey published a Name Book with the following description of Biggar – *'Small town consisting of one wide street nearly half a mile in length and very irregular, there are several low, thatched tenements in the town, but the buildings are generally two storeys plain and slated'*.

A major enhancement came to the street in 1887 when, for Queen Victoria's jubilee, a fountain was installed outside the Corn Exchange and two rows of trees were planted along the street edges. More recent 'improvements' took place in 1970 and 1998. 1970 saw the loss of the Cairngryffe red felsite surface on the main carriageway and the iron cages around the trees. New chestnut , ash and sycamore trees were planted at this time. More formal parking was installed in 1998 and many more trees were replaced.

South (shady) side

Nos 2, 4 and 6 High St. The Biggar Burgh records of June 1869 record a house and shops being built at West End beside the bridge. They were built by James Brown, Candy Cottage (No 8). No 2 was the business of James Brunton, grocer from 1874. Lindsay Bros, painters, started business in 1876 in one of the attics before moving further up the street; George Kerr, builder, began married life in another. James Brunton had a big family and was succeeded by John Brunton, his son whose name stayed above the door until the 1990s. Ed and Jimmy Pretswell worked tirelessly here in the war years and after and the business later belonged to Ed's son Edmund who bought out his aunt, Jimmy's widow. Some of Brunton's tea bins are on display in the Biggar and Upper Clydesdale Museum.

Thomas Mitchell, the saddler, was at No 4 in 1875 but moved further up and across to No 67 around 1900. Abernethy the butcher was in this shop till about the end of the first world war when it became John Fergus's bookshop (1920) and had a sign painted in futuristic lettering by his friend DG Millar.

Biggar High Street 1857, 1:2500

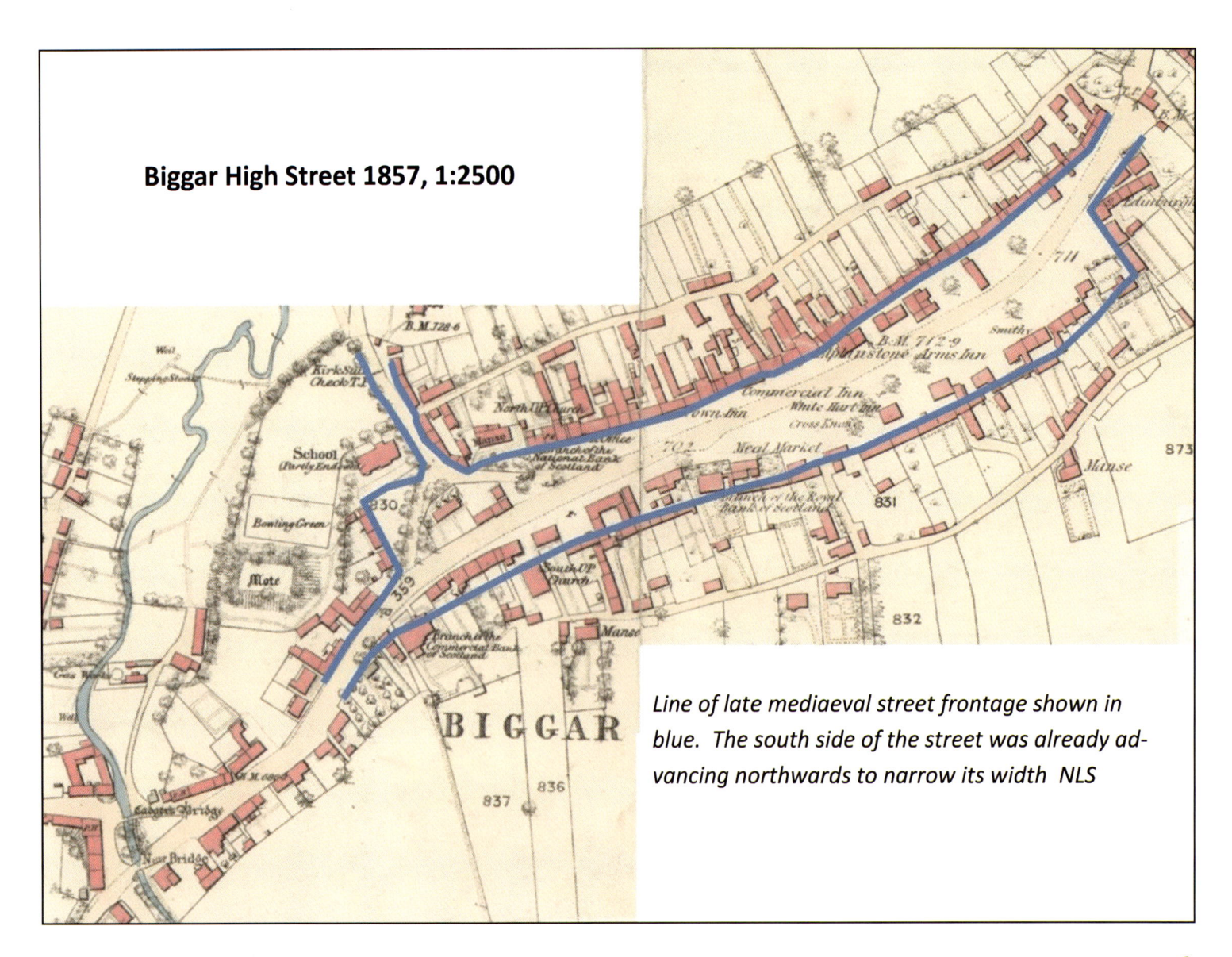

Line of late mediaeval street frontage shown in blue. The south side of the street was already advancing northwards to narrow its width NLS